The Leader-Mind Equation

The Leader-Mind Equation

Mindful Choices for Effective Leaders

Rob Stones

The Leader-Mind Equation

Mindful Choices for Effective Leaders

First published 2020.

Author: Rob Stones

Editor: Valerie Stones

Image Creator: Jeremy Stones

Copyright to this work is asserted by:
Rob Stones of FutureShape Consulting

No portion of this book may be reproduced or printed without permission.

ISBN: 978-0-646-82160-3
©FutureShape Consulting, 2020. All Rights Reserved.

This book is dedicated to my wife, Valerie.

Without her encouragement to actually finish the writing I had started, the material on these pages would still be scattered through a dozen dusty notebooks.

In so far as the book is easy to read and understand, it is due to Val's meticulous attention to detail as an editor.

This is my heartfelt 'thank you' for five decades of love and inspiration.

TABLE OF CONTENTS

	INTRODUCTION	5
	SECTION ONE	
-	**CHAPTER ONE – THE MIND OF A LEADER**	
1.1	The search for Magic	10
1.2	Mind and Brain	12
1.3	Effectively leading minds	14
1.4	Every Mind is a control system	15
1.5	Lead to get the effect you want	17
-	**CHAPTER TWO – THE PARADOX OF POWER**	
2.1	The limits of leadership effectiveness	19
2.2	No-one can command commitment	22
2.3	I am the only person I can control	23
-	**CHAPTER THREE - LEADERSHIP LEARNING**	
3.1	The orders of leadership effectiveness	27
3.2	Leaders who manage self, show the way	31
	SECTION TWO	
-	**CHAPTER FOUR – MOTIVATION AND THE MIND**	
4.1	To manage self, know self	34
4.2	The three operations of the mind	36
4.3	The mind that looks after itself	39
4.4	Motivation	40
4.5	Choosing the WANT we pay attention to	44
4.6	NEEDS – the unseen foundations of motive	47
4.7	The need for AUTONOMY	51
4.8	Avoiding Pain	52
4.9	implications for leaders	54
-	**CHAPTER FIVE – PERCEPTION: THE INPUT PROCESS**	
5.1	The deceptive practice of perception	57
5.2	The knowledge lens creates beliefs	59
5.3	The values lens	61
5.4	Implications for Leaders	63
-	**CHAPTER SIX – BEHAVING**	
6.1	Behaving: the output process	66

6.2	The metaphor of the car	68
6.3	Managing our behaviours	70
6.4	Habits	71
6.5	Leadership behaviours	73
6.6	The work of the mind: a summary	76

SECTION THREE

CHAPTER SEVEN – KNOWING WHAT YOU WANT

7.1	Knowing what you want	79
7.2	What the effective leader wants	81
7.3	Knowing what you really want matters	82
7.4	Why is the real want not obvious?	85
7.5	Beware the intrusion of the 'don't want'	87
7.6	Effective leadership is always on the scales	90
7.7	Delaying gratification	93

CHAPTER EIGHT – RESPONSIBILITY

8.1	Accepting responsibility	95
8.2	The alternative: out of control	97
8.3	The consequences of evading responsibility	99
8.4	The two choices	100

CHAPTER NINE – SELF-EVALUATION

9.1	No failure, only feedback!	102
9.2	The procedures for self-enhancement	103
9.3	Achieving clarity	105
9.4	Self-evaluating	107
9.5	Review options, make a choice, take action	109

SECTION FOUR

CHAPTER TEN – THE PRE-REQUISITE FOR EFFECTIVENESS

10.1	The effectiveness equation	112
10.2	Capable skills plus excitement plus practice	115
10.3	Building Capacity	116
10.4	Four mind-tools of capability	118
10.5	Emotions	119
10.6	Self-talk	121
10.7	Mental Imaging – the pictures in our heads	125
10.8	Self-concept: how we see ourselves	126

Chapter Eleven – The Generic Capabilities 1

11.1	Perceptual agility	131
11.2	Zooming Out	134

Chapter Twelve – The Generic Capabilities 2

12.1	Coaching	138
12.3	Coach the way the mind works - an example	140
12.3	Features of a successful coaching conversation	145
12.4	The want must be positive	146
12.5	Gaining clarity about the want	149
12.6	The importance of paraphrasing	150
12.7	Self-evaluation is the fulcrum	152
12.8	Another example coaching conversation	154

Chapter Thirteen - The Generic Capabilities 3

13.1	Creating Team	160
13.2	A team requires 'teaming'	161
13.3	What team is	162
13.4	Formulating shared purpose	163
13.5	The I in team	164
13.6	Identifying and nurturing interdependence	166
13.7	Consensus decision making	168
13.8	Using coaching questions	171
13.10	Encouraging open conversation	171
13.11	Constructive dispute and deep thinking	175

Chapter Fourteen – Direction (not directives)

14.1	Knowing where to tap	178
14.2	Directing our efforts	183
14.3	Shared Direction – The Window of Certainty©	185
14.4	The vision frame	188
14.5	The outcomes frame	193
14.6	The beliefs frame	196
14.7	The values frame	201
14.8	The window of certainty encourages autonomy	205
14.9	The leader as a boundary rider	206
14.10	The boundary conversation	208
14.11	There must be a bottom line!	214

Chapter Fifteen – Commitment

15.1	Where commitment fits	217
15.2	From disengaged to committed	219
15.3	The real motives of human behaviour	223
15.4	Misconceptions about motivation	224
15.5	Willingness	226
15.6	Creating opportunities for intrinsic motivation	231
15.7	Autonomy supportive conditions	232
15.8	Achievement supportive conditions	234
15.9	The conditions for satisfying relationships	236
15.10	The conditions for meaningful learning	238
15.11	Safe conditions	241
15.12	Meaningful Contribution	243

Chapter Sixteen – Minus Distractions!

16.1	Hindrances to unrelenting focus	248
16.2	Politics	250
16.3	Stuck in self	251
16.4	The heady wine of hubris	253
16.5	Wriggling from responsibility	255
16.6	Liking and disliking	258
16.7	Indulging emotions	260
16.8	Self-protection	261
16.9	The blindness of bosses	263
16.10	Linear thinking	265
16.11	The systems trap	266
16.12	Not training for tomorrow	269

Chapter Seventeen – Conclusion

17.1	One lighthouse or many candles?	272
17.2	The effectiveness formula	277
17.3	Are you willing?	279

Notes and References		282

INTRODUCTION

This book has been written for those who want to understand, develop, and discipline their own mental processes in order to be the most effective leader that they can be.

There is no phrase that denotes this kind of attending to and nurturing your own cognition in order to lead more effectively, so I invented one. I call it *Leader-Mind*.

The nature of leadership and the development of leaders is often obscured by out-of-date mind-science. Leader behaviours based on the notion that people can be controlled, and anecdotes about adventitious success, tend to take centre stage in the daily, often contradictory, practice of leaders who do not understand or manage their own minds.

In this book, leader effectiveness is the focus. Leadership behaviours, based on an enlightened but simple understanding of how the mind works, will help those in executive positions to tune their thinking in order to inspire the best out of those whom they lead. The leader's role is to improve the performance of the organisation through the people who work in it: to ensure that both the team and the business are optimally effective.

Effectiveness always starts with the leader's understanding of self. For many years, I have asserted and explained that self-management is the first action requirement for leaders. Without this primary commitment to leading self, nobody will be well-led.

When you are committed to acquiring *Leader-Mind,* you will manage your own thinking processes and attendant behaviours in order to produce the most productive results possible for your team or enterprise. Becoming *Leader-Minded,* in order to be effective in your role, is what this book is about.

There is a quality of mindful deliberation which stamps the best, most effective leaders apart from others. I don't believe it is innate – in fact I am certain that it's not. This kind of thinking is learned.

It can be learned by leaders at any level, but it often isn't. Its principles are relatively simple: understand your own mental processes, manage them, calibrate their outputs and keep adjusting them to get effective results. Despite the simplicity of this, many people who are appointed to leadership roles prefer to act from their instincts or draw on redundant theories of human behaviour and change. They don't learn that the first step is to understand and manage their own cognitive processes. The only mind we have access to is our own. Only when we are aware of how our own mental processing works can we presume to apply this knowledge to others.

Whatever is your present level of leadership, whether you are an adept or a novice, I hope that you have opened these pages with a willingness to learn and adopt practices and skills in order

MINDFUL CHOICES FOR EFFECTIVE LEADERS

to be even more effective. Leadership is an extraordinary vocation; one that brings substantial satisfaction but demands effort, learning and continuous personal change.

I spent a substantial portion of my life learning to be a leader - and a subsequent chunk of later life working out that I, like almost everyone else, could have been better at it.

The formula for success as a leader has four elements:
1. A set of cognitive and leadership behaviours learned to the level of capable use;
2. A clear purpose and direction with which to apply them;
3. Commitment to giving priority to being *Leader-Minded* in enhancing your team or organisation;
4. Willingness to manage the myriad distractions, from within and without, that can interfere with your clarity of thinking.

Think of it as an equation:

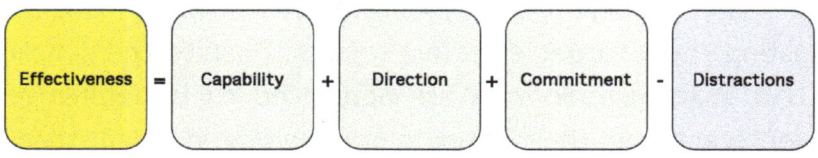

The structure of the book expands on and clarifies this equation:

Section One – Effective Leadership

Chapters 1 to 3 — Deals with some critical elements of effectiveness in the leader's role. What is the nature of leadership effectiveness and why does it matter?

Chapters 4 to 6	**Section Two – The Effective Mind** Explores the way that the mind works and explains how our perceiving process, decision-making and subsequent behaviours work, and the implications of these for leadership.
Chapters 7 to 9	**Section Three – Leader-Mind Capabilities** Introduces the three practices that are the crux of mind-management, the critical reflection and learning tools that are central to becoming *Leader-Minded*.
Chapters 10 to 16	**Section Four – The Formula in Detail.** Is devoted to exploring the four elements of the Effectiveness Formula and the cognitive and behavioural tools that are enhanced when you develop *Leader-Mind*.

Many years of talking with, and listening to, leaders at all levels have helped me to refine and present the ways in which a leader, by managing his or her own mind, can reach the highest levels of proficiency. This book is my contribution to those who aspire to effective and ennobling leadership and are humble enough to learn what it takes.

Although I am presenting a very personal approach to the enterprise of leadership, it is widely researched in three senses:
- Wherever possible in my own leadership career and as a teacher of leaders, I learned from the scholarship, experience and wisdom of others and from the insights of the research community.

- As a practising leader, I learned from the many mistakes I made.[1] We often pay lip service to the learning that we can get from trying, failing and reflecting. But I have lived it! This research-in-action approach has helped me to understand how to lead with a clarity that can only be achieved by getting it wrong many times!
- Thirdly, in my present occupation as a leadership consultant and trainer, I have tested and refined these ideas in the context of hundreds of workshops and conversations. This has enabled me to draw on the practical wisdom and leadership nous of the many people who have been willing to explore and discuss their experiences with me.

Talking about leadership and how to develop effective leader behaviours is how I now spend my time. The writer Haruki Murakami,[2] an author whose hobby is running, titled one of his books *What I talk about when I talk about running.* The subject of this book is not running but leading. The topic may be different, but my approach is the same. In these pages I am exploring the themes that form '*what I talk about when I talk about leading.*'

The opinions and ideas that I have sought and drawn upon - in conversations I have had with others over the last 20 years - have continually challenged and clarified my own thinking. If what follows makes sense, it is because it is the product of many minds, not just my own.

Chapter One

The MIND of a Leader

"In the realms of radical optimism, the search for a magic bullet goes on endlessly. In the no-nonsense life of the leader, it is best to rely on learning."

RG Pierre [1]

1.1
The Search for Magic?

We live in a world where it's increasingly common to use devices or gadgets and their 'apps' to access the tools that can simplify or accelerate our work in the interest of greater effectiveness (at least that's what we yearn for!)
Imagine that, in the spirit of this world view, I was to offer you a quite remarkable device: one with astonishing processing power in terms of speed, range and flexibility, equipped with a phenomenal memory.

This appliance can reconfigure itself according to the user's experience and, in keeping with the most sophisticated software available, make value judgments about the 'likes' and aversions of the user in every dimension of their life.

An extraordinary feature of this device, a kind of 'Super-App', is its ability to emanate packets of energy that can be sensed and processed by the people around you. The data is transmitted as sound, light, physical sensation, smell, taste or even manifested in some mysterious way so that it can be received intuitively.

Of course, the data transmitted has to be received and interpreted by the intended recipients, but (and here's the real genius of this device) in the hands of a skilful user, the appliance is able to tune itself to the input processes of other people and influence how they interpret the data they receive.

The device (with its apps) can't actually control other people, but if the user learns to use them with sensitivity and discernment they can be adjusted and applied in ways that spread the influence of the user far and wide…..

….. Enough - the metaphor will only take us so far because, of course, you possess such a device – or rather, you **are** *that device.*

1.2
MIND AND BRAIN: THE GHOST IN THE MACHINE

As a human, you **are** a control system: a sophisticated organism that can be used more or less competently to achieve the goals of the user – that's you!

Your brain (which includes neurons all over your body, not just in your head) has 20 billion nerve cells which can fire up to 200 times per second. The latest research shows that each dendrite (that's the branching piece at the end of the axons of every cell) is itself a minicomputer. That means that you can make use of the processing capacity of 20-million-billion potential connections that are at your brain's disposal. Too many noughts to process at a conscious level! And of course, the human brain is capable of parallel processing (working at many levels at once), which is something we have not yet been able to design a computer to do.

We don't have direct access to the management of our brain activity. We experience the brain as MIND. Our mental processes are the conscious manifestations of the activity of the nervous system – how we code the activity of the brain in ways that are accessible to thought. All of that neural activity is constantly whizzing along, but the consciousness that arises from its activity 'appears to us' as the working of our minds.

We can't directly manage the activity of our billions of neural connections, but we can manage our own accessible representations of that activity. That's why it's 'managing the mind' that we will be talking about in this book.

Fundamentally, the mind performs its activity through three different operations: it takes in information from the world around us; processes it by comparing our present perception with what we want; and then creates the decision as a behaviour which is intended to make things better for us, or to protect us. There are a whole lot of caveats and complexities attached to those basic operations, but these are the 3 activities that are at the heart of it:
- Taking in information (perceiving);
- Internal processing (thinking or comparing);
- Behaving.

It is these three operations, the effects that flow from managing them deliberately and the significance of this self-control for leadership that I am going to explore in these pages.

At this stage, I want to emphasise two important features of how the mind works:
1. The mind is an internal control system: it controls the behaviours of our biological self;
2. It can be managed intentionally or allowed to run on autopilot (habit).

Clearly, I am contending that intentional mind-management is the better choice!

1.3
EFFECTIVELY LEADING MINDS

If our mind is a control system, managing our own behaviours from moment to moment, then everyone has such a system. When we refer to leading other people, we are leading other minds.

In my work with leaders, I often use the *Leader-Mind* equation help us to remain focused on what matters in leadership:

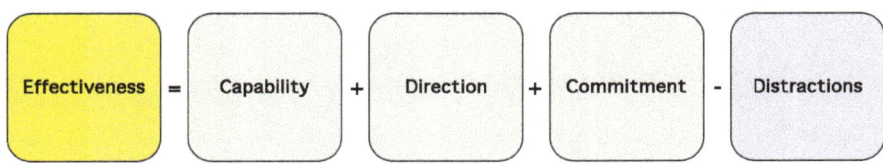

If this formula is to make sense, then we had better start by defining what effectiveness in leadership is:
1. A successful leader will capably apply learnable skills to influence and enhance the behaviours, capacity and commitment of the people they lead;[2]
2. This leadership influence will make a positive difference to the success or performance of the team, organisation or enterprise which the leader heads.

In other words, the effective leader helps others to optimise both their capacity and commitment in order that the organisation will thrive.

It is easy to objectify people as 'staff' or 'team members' or 'employees', and then to speak and act as if they were members of a class or set which can in some way be managed by systems or processes or rules. Thinking like this misleads us;

it obscures the reality. Whoever you lead, then you are leading individual people - people with minds. However numerous the minds we lead, it is individual minds that respond to us - or resist us. To be *Leader-Minded* is to be relentlessly aware that we are leading minds: minds that work in the same way as our own.

An effective leader knows that they are leading other people who are interpreting and evaluating everything that the leader does or says. It's the mind of each individual that will be inspired by the leader's words and actions - or resist them!

1.4
EVERY MIND IS AN INTERNAL CONTROL SYSTEM

One of the assumptions that permeates language, and which creates a great deal of wasted energy and misery, is that we can be controlled from outside ourselves: that we can do things **to** other people to make them behave in certain ways; or that **they** can control us by their actions.

Of course, other people do or say things which we process through our own perceptual system, and we naturally include this information in our internal processing. Without question, events and experiences occur which we perceive as painful or pleasurable, and which affect the way we think and behave. But they don't *'CAUSE'* how we behave. To paraphrase Victor Frankl[3]:

*"Between **stimulus** and **response** there is a **space**. In that **space** is our power to **choose our response**. In that choice lies our growth and our freedom."*

If we put this into a diagram, if we observe a person from the outside the link between cause and effect may look like this:

But it takes only a brief examination of our internal experience to know that what is really happening is this:

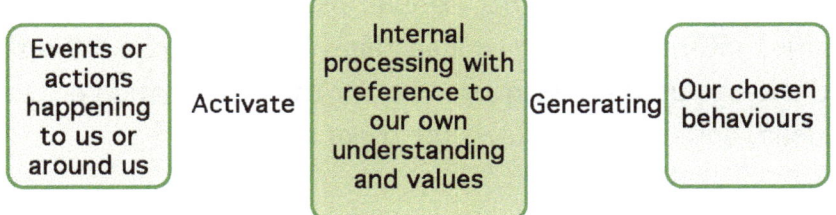

The internal processing may be automated (a habit) or unconscious. But, except when we act instinctively after sudden pain or threat, there is an internal process that separates the external experience and the behaviour we respond with. Most of this book is about how we can become more aware of and manage that experience, and why doing so is important.

The critical significance of understanding that everyone is internally controlled in this way is that it brings with it the realisation that nothing **we** can do can **make** anyone else do anything.

As leaders, we can control our own behaviours so that what other people experience as a result will influence them. We can learn from the results of our own behaviours and, when we don't achieve the effect or influence we hope for, we can change our words or actions and try something else. In other words, we can manage and control our own behaviours directly, but our only influence on others is the result of how well we manage ourselves!

1.5
LEAD TO GET THE **EFFECT** YOU WANT

When we are leading other people, most of us do this with a positive intent: we want to lead them in a way that will result in the best outcome for ourselves, for the organisation or team we lead, and, almost always, for them as well.

When we understand how the human mind (the human control system) works, we can quite deliberately manage ourselves in ways that maximise the likelihood that our behaviours will help our staff to do their best work.

I emphasise again - we cannot control or motivate other people. As an internal control system, each person is motivated from the inside. *But*, with some important knowledge about how the human mind works, and with a commitment to learn to manage our own mind, we can behave in ways that will be influential and even inspiring for others.

This means that we will thrive as leaders if we view our own mind as if it were that powerful and sensitive device that we referred to at the start of this section. If we commit to learning

how to use and calibrate our mind and manage the way in which it generates our behaviours, we are more likely to get the results that we want to achieve.
Not everyone is willing to do this.

Some leaders treat their own brain as if it was a megaphone attached to a recording device! They press 'play' and out comes the stuff that they think other people should think and do, delivered at full opinionated volume. If they notice that the people receiving their output are responding with resistance or low-level compliance, then they blame the receivers, not the output. This is the pathway to frustration and ineffectiveness.

Dr. William Glasser[4] reminded us of a piece of wisdom that helps us to avoid this frustration: "The only person we can control is our own self."

When we fully accept this truth, when we make a decision to base our thought and actions upon it, then we can embark on the journey of personal learning and discipline that will result in leadership effectiveness: the management of our own mind.

Mind management is about learning to use the 'device' that is ourselves with increasing degrees of sophistication and effectiveness. We can learn to use it well or lazily: to pay attention to our own perceptions, processing and behaviour and to calibrate these in order to get the responses we want – or not. It's a choice.

In the next chapter, we will look at one of the key reasons why that choice is crucial to leadership effectiveness.

Chapter Two

THE PARADOX OF LEADERSHIP POWER

"Leaders become great, not because of their own power, but because of their ability to empower others."

John C Maxwell[1]

2.1
THE LIMITS OF LEADERSHIP EFFECTIVENESS

If this book is to be 'real' it has to be exceptionally clear about the limitations of leadership. True recognition of those limitations is, I believe, the key to unleashing the power of the leader's most potent asset – his or her ability to manage self in order to encourage, inspire and empower other people.

Whatever kind of organisation we lead, unless it's a one-person enterprise, success will ultimately depend on the productive work and energised commitment of the people we lead.

Whether we recognise it and accept it or spend our working life railing against it (and some do!), all leaders are largely dependent for their effectiveness on the performance of other people in their organisation.

As leaders who want to experience success, embracing this paradox is more than important - it is pivotal!

Unless we can achieve the results or productivity we strive to create on our own (and we rarely can), then dependence on the skills, abilities and gifts of others is a 'given'. It's the people we lead who produce our product, engage our clients, lead the learning and make our enterprise exceptional. With a line-up of high performing staff, every leader is gifted the keys to effectiveness.

This element of dependence, this inconvenient 'law of reliance'[2], is the actuality and the paradox at the heart of leadership.

For many of us, this comes as an unpleasant revelation. It's confronting that at that point in our careers when we seem to have been vested with significant authority, we discover that our ability to be in command is an illusion. A prized external measure of our personal capability - the elevation in our status to a leadership role - turns out to be far different from our expectation. The assumption that position power would be associated with increased control over people and events turns out to be a mirage!

In the world of authentic experience, this uncomfortable reality soon becomes apparent. We accept responsibility for the quality and productivity of other people's work, and with this comes the obligation we feel to deliver meritorius outcomes. But we soon realise that we have little direct control of what our people may do to achieve results.

The frustrations that go with this realisation are commonplace – and understandable. It seems unreasonable for anyone in a position of responsibility to be relatively powerless – dependent on their subordinates for success. It seems like a formula for creating discontent!

However, most of us soon learn that expressing our frustration by increasing our efforts to control and manipulate our team members only takes us deeper into the contradiction.

This is where the second element of the paradox at the heart of the leader's challenge kicks in.

**People can never be <u>made</u>
to do what we want them to do.**

Remember: everyone is internally controlled. Of course, up to a point, we can use our position power to insist on their compliance – or at least the appearance of it. Often our colleagues are not so bold as to challenge us directly. If we put our foot down and insist on obedience, then our staff will usually go along with us to keep their jobs or to keep the peace.

In public, our position power may result in acquiescence, and any resistance will become passive. However, for reasons that are explored later in the book, compliance comes with a corresponding decrease in the creative engagement of our staff.

The problem is that trying to control the behaviour of other people by overpowering them actually creates resistance. Coercion can never tap into the wellsprings of human motivation or encourage high quality work and commitment. The under-appreciated biological law that emerges in human behaviour is written starkly in the annals of history:

If you push me, I will push back!

2.2
No-one can command Commitment

As Michael Fullan[3] puts it, "You can't mandate what matters."

We are all familiar with the harmful pre-supposition that we can manage the behaviour of other people using external control: i.e. we can make people do things. It is embedded in language, and in 'common-sense' parenting, schooling and politics. It carries with it three harmful diseases of the thought process that cause havoc in human interaction and relationships:
1. Other people can be made to do things;
2. Because I am a leader, it is my right to make other people do as I want;

3. Therefore, I have a responsibility to do whatever is required to make other people behave as I want them to.

This is the tyrant trap! These 'thought diseases', although they offer the promise of control, actually diminish our influence over the people we work with. This is where the paradox of leadership power really bites us. In basing our work with others on the assumption that we can and should control other people, we can easily damage our actual influence on them.

Influence is a delicate instrument based on perception and relationships. It is the perception of the people we lead that matters: the degree of trust and respect that they have for us is critical to the degree of influence that we have with them.

If we don't understand or heed the significance of the internal decision-making processes that are going on in the minds of the staff we lead, then we can find ourselves using the very strategies that will make things worse rather than better.

2.3
I AM THE ONLY PERSON THAT I CAN CONTROL

This is why the psychology of human behaviour and motivation is 'MUST KNOW' information and understanding for leaders.

We do know that we can exert considerable control over our own behaviour. The more we practise it, the better we get at it. But this ability to control self is not an analogy for the degree of control we can have over other people. The mechanism of influence is very different. We can manage our own behaviour to closely match our perfect picture of how we should be. We can't manage other people by requiring them to behave as **we** would like.

If we go down the 'command and control' track, instead of inspiring and enthusing our team members, we will initiate relationships in which minimal compliance or passive resistance are common responses to leadership demand: the staff are expected to do as they are told because we say so. But there is no energy, no commitment, no unleashing of personal power in 'compliance'.

Imagine how effective you would be as the manager of a sporting team if most of your team took the field do no more than to comply with the coach's instructions – with no personal skill or creativity, judgment or initiative to draw upon!

Peter Drucker[4], cutting to the heart of the matter as always, reminded us to that "to get the best from the people we work with, we will do best if we treat every one of them as if they were a volunteer". It may seem as if (unlike volunteers who can walk away at any time) most people need their job. However, the truth that Drucker points towards is that if their hearts walk away, so does an enormous percentage of the potential energy and commitment that they bring to our organisation.

Effective leaders always remember that they are leaders and not commanders, and that as responsibilities increase and the size of the staff expands, the leader's effectiveness becomes increasingly dependent on the productivity and capability of the members of the team.

This is the significance of the central paradox of leadership. Leaders are responsible for outcomes, but in order to achieve them must become 'debtors' to the staff they lead.[5]

So, on the one hand, our job as a leader is to point the way: to establish and promote virtuous and productive goals; to build capacity; to set the agenda with which the organisation will flourish. Yet on the other hand, because we are dependent on the commitment, energy and the quality of work of our 'followers', we have to think very deeply about **how** to achieve this.

Because in every team and organisation it is the employees' effectiveness that leads to the success of the enterprise, the only way that a business can truly thrive is by enhancing the capabilities of the men and women who do the work. The challenge for leaders is to channel their leadership endeavours into finding ways to create an exceptional work force. Leader effectiveness only emerges when we are surrounded by the efficacy of others.

This is not in any way to minimize the importance of leaders: effective leadership is almost always a pre-condition for the emergence and development of high-performing staff. Leaders may depend on their employees, but it is also true that outstanding practitioners are most likely to emerge in the presence of good leaders.

What these twin realities do bring to the fore is the importance of balancing the two poles of the leadership paradox. The more that the workers on whose performance we depend are encouraged to thrive, the more likely it is that we will be successful as leaders.

When we put together the elements of the paradox of power - that our job is to promote and engender capability and effectiveness in our team, but without being able to mandate this level of human commitment - we come face to face with the nature of leadership.

Effective leaders are those who:
- Know that the only person they can control is themselves;
- Understand that power and authority are mostly illusion and usually elusive. Position on the org. chart does not vest a person with the capacity to be effective;
- Understand enough about human behaviour and motivation to know how to encourage the growth of capability and personal growth in their team;
- Can put this knowledge into practice by influencing and engaging those whom they lead.

Leaders are the promoters of productive action. It's our professional business to learn everything that is needed to enhance the productivity of our organisation.

Chapter Three

The Pattern of Leadership Learning

"A leader is a person you will follow to a place you wouldn't go by yourself."

Warren Bennis

3.1
The 'Orders' of Leadership Effectiveness

The framework on the next page illustrates the four 'orders' of leader effectiveness:

1. When a leader is sufficiently able to manage their thoughts, emotions and behaviour, they will learn to behave in ways that will be most likely to influence those around them;

> Influencing and managing self through cognitive and emotional self-regulation
>
> Influencing and encouraging others in order to develop high levels of autonomous commitment
>
> Forming and maintaining teams with shared purpose and ideals within a collaborative culture
>
> Strategic leadership of change through understanding and use of complex processes and systems that contribute to organisational effectiveness

The 'Leader-Mind Matrix', FutureShape Consulting 2011[2]

2. When this influence is established, they are able to initiate and nurture capability around themselves;
3. As individual autonomy and capability grow, the capacity to build collaborative, high-performing teams emerges. A culture of interdependence and value-based cohesion can then develop around shared mental models;
4. Within this culture, the attention to evidence-informed strategy and systems produces growing creativity and productivity. The organisation draws on its growing capacity and the synergy of creative individuals to manage complexity and to experience mutual success.

I describe these as the 'orders' of leadership effectiveness because they almost always correspond to the sequence in which a leader's potency emerges.

Unless the first order - self-management - is mastered, the ability to establish the kind of influence that will make a difference to the capacity and performance of others will often be hit-and-miss.

The importance of the first order is its impact on the conditions needed for the next order to emerge and so on. For example, unless the leader is managing themselves well enough to be predictable, displays understanding and consideration to others, and is transparent about their purpose, they are unlikely to be trusted. Until they are seen to model the behaviours they expect from others, while encouraging and appreciating the efforts of team members, few staff will take the risk of investing time and energy to commit to their cause. To embrace the higher levels of challenge that will lead to personal and professional growth, most people need a leader who will on the one hand provide opportunity, and on the other will appreciate that temporary failure is the necessary companion of learning. This does need some self-management at times!

Each of the other 'orders' of leadership is similarly dependent on the one above.

All of this is significant because leading is not 'being in charge'. All organisations have 'fashions' in the use of language. Nowadays, everyone in a position of responsibility tends to be described as a 'leader' or an 'executive' whatever they actually contribute to the organisation. But it's not the name that I want to pay attention to here, it's the function.

There are lots of terms for those whose role involves managing the work of others. We can call them managers or supervisors or bosses. They all tend to refer to the same relationship: a person who is responsible for overseeing or administering the work of other people.

This is not the work of a leader. Leaders are people whose job is to step into a place that is better than the present and take other people with them.

As Warren Bennis[3] wrote so succinctly: "The Manager accepts the status quo; the Leader challenges it".

Now this is not to deny that most of us in leadership roles also have a role in managing, reporting, supervising and clerical activity. There are many days when the work of leadership is overwhelmed by the administrative necessities of the role. However, if we see ourselves as primarily leaders, even during those times when we are busy with managerial tasks, the knowledge that leadership is our primary role can, as we will see, fundamentally change the way we go about the business of managing or supervising.

3.2
LEADERS MANAGE SELF TO SHOW THE WAY

As you will have seen from the previous chapters, this book has a lot to say about the limitations of being a leader: the things that we can't do as leaders (even though we wish we could). But I think it's important to establish that vigorous leadership is essential to an effective organisation.

The key job of the leader comes at the second and third orders of leadership effectiveness, which is to nurture other leaders. Inevitably, in a well-led organisation, the capability, initiative and enterprise of others will emerge and flourish.

Experience tells us that the enterprising collaboration of a team of people working together can, and does, produce a transformative groundswell of 'bottom-up' initiative. However, for this to happen, teams have to be formed and brought together in a unifying culture of effectiveness.

These things don't happen without the initiation of a leader. RG Pierre[4] is wont to remind me that it's easy to identify effective leaders: they leave a trail of capability in their wake!

A significant improvement in the performance of an enterprise rarely occurs spontaneously: it is most likely to emerge when the leader has done the work required to prise open the gates of possibility.

The words of Lin Yutang[5] are a powerful parable for the importance of the leader: *"Hope is like a road in the country;*

there was never a road, but when many people walk on it, the road comes into existence."

The different approach, the unheralded potential, the way forward that most people can't see, becomes visible when a leader dares to pioneer it, invites other people to join them on that path or, most powerfully of all, liberates others to forge the path themselves.

Jean-Paul Sartre[6] described imagination as 'the ability to think of what is not'. It is this capability which is the hallmark of leading. Lin Yutang's powerful metaphor captures the essence of the work of those who want to lead instead of (perhaps as well as) manage. The leader's imagination ushers hope into the conversations of the enterprise.

There is a cost to this of course! The price that leaders pay for seeing and initiating the changes that enrich their staff or team is that they do have to put up with the initial doubt and cynicism of those who don't believe that 'the invisible road' exists. Pioneers are always exposed to the barbs of others when they forge ahead. Only after they have courageously gone ahead, and others have followed; when "the road comes into existence", does this courage pay off.

Here is yet another paradoxical feature of leadership. Unless the leader is willing to stand out, take the risks associated with promoting a vision that others can't yet see, then only the status quo remains.

But, at the same time, leaders can't become isolated. The road will never emerge if it is trodden alone. The leader's job is to initiate change and exploration in ways that encourage others to join, and to bring their very best to the journey that they will then walk together.

All too often, leaders have to dance on the edge of their own helplessness - yet still calm their own mind - in order to generate enough trust and belief to energise the performance of others.

Acquiring *Leader-Mind* is my description of the focus of the self-managing leader: the person who can manage their own mind well enough to step into this challenging space.

Developing *Leader-Mind* is effortful. However, this level of mindful self-management is enabled by a thorough understanding of the way in which the mind works. It's for this reason that the next section is devoted to an explanation of how our minds actually function.

SECTION TWO

CHAPTER FOUR

MOTIVATION AND THE MIND

"Based on experiences in our lives, we select images and experiences that represent to us the highest quality that we can imagine at that moment - and try to achieve this quality."

Barnes Boffey[1]

4.1
TO MANAGE SELF - KNOW SELF

There are two important reasons why we who lead others should understand human behaviour and motivation:
- Firstly, so that we can learn how to manage ourselves in ways that are most likely to influence and inspire the behaviour of the people around us;

- Secondly, so that we can understand and appreciate the behaviours of the people we lead, and we can choose the behaviours which are most likely to encourage them to become engaged with, and committed to, the work we are doing together.

In this section, I want to present the best simple explanation I know about how the human mind works. Throughout the book, I will tease out the powerful implications of this explanation through the many dimensions of the leader's work.

Leaders who do not trouble to understand the working of the mind are often perplexed by the behaviour and resistance of their staff; their reluctance to engage with the leader's agenda. They struggle to find a productive response to the frustrations inherent in these common conflicts of influence and understanding.

Knowledge of the underlying psychology of human behaviour and motivation is the key to recognising and managing our own behaviour. It also provides us with helpful insight into the minds of others so that we can connect with and influence them.

The human mind, with all of its complexities, performs three operations, all of which are used to process and respond to the world around us.

Firstly, we take in information from the world around us. This is an active process that is not the passive receipt of data but a process of translation and interpretation[2].

Secondly, we make choices about what to do with the information we take in. This deciding process involves *comparing* what we perceive from moment to moment with our unique representations of what we want.

Thirdly, we generate a behaviour with which we intend to close the gap between what we are perceiving and what we want. Some of this behaviour (such as our actions) is visible to others. Other elements of our behaviour (such as thinking) can be relatively invisible unless we make them so.

4.2
THE THREE OPERATIONS OF THE MIND

We might illustrate these three operations performed by the human mind like this:

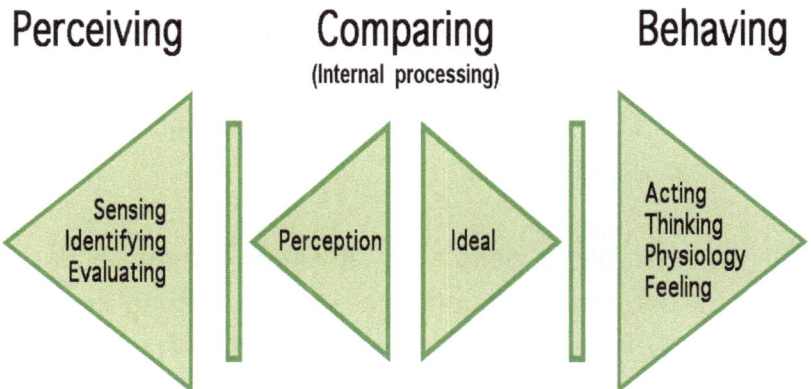

In effect, there is a great deal of overlap between the three functions. However, I will present them as though they are distinct from each other and will explore the significance of the interaction between the processes at a later point.

The primary source of the explanation I present below is Dr. William Glasser's Choice Theory®[3], to which I have added insights gleaned from other sources such as Self Determination Theory [4], NLP [5], neuroscience writers David Rock[6] and Norman Doidge[7], and the worldwide positive psychology community[8].

At its most simple, the brain is our control system. What we call 'mind' is the representation of brain activity in our awareness. The brain itself is like the CPU of the human organism - the hardware that processes our experiences. Our thoughts, feelings, emotions; our attitudes, beliefs and values, memories and imaginings are our mental representations of the electrical and chemical activity in the neural circuits of the brain. We might compare them to the software that runs on the system.

When we consider our mental experiences, it's common knowledge that preferring pleasure to pain is a design feature of our biological nature: we are created to avoid pain and maximise pleasant or satisfying experience. But what is not well understood is that it is our INTERNAL experience of pleasure and pain that is significant.

It may be that other people do at times intend to hurt us. Sometimes people try to influence us by offering something that they believe will please us. And, of course, the circumstances and events of our lives sometimes bring us pain. But our response to these people and events is rarely predictable. There is a reason for this: because we control our behaviour to optimise our feelings of INTERNAL pleasure, or to avoid INTERNAL pain, things are rarely what they seem from the outside. The human control system is calibrated to respond to what we are experiencing internally, not to react to the observable experience.

This failure to understand that human behaviour is internally, not externally, generated runs deep in the library of faulty human assumptions. It leads to the common but erroneous belief that we can control people by punishing them or rewarding them. But much as we prefer to avoid pain, many of us hate the pain of being controlled and manipulated most of all - and that applies to manipulative rewards as well to punitive behaviours that are intended to hurt us. I know this first-hand because I reacted to attempts to control me manipulatively quite early in my life.

I was educated in an era which believed in the power of punishment – and it was indeed intended to hurt us! The use of the cane was commonplace. In my secondary school in East Africa, hitting children with a length of bamboo was used for encouragement as well as for transgression! At this school, staffed by men and women recruited from English 'Public Schools'[9], I was introduced for the first time to Latin. A bewildered 12-year old, I made a very poor attempt at my first Latin homework. When I failed the subsequent test, I received 2 strokes of the cane to encourage me to try harder next time. It had the opposite effect. I obstinately refused to make any attempt to learn the hated language[10]!

Of course, I knew nothing about the psychology of motivation in those days. What I did know was that I was not going to submit to unfair treatment. I hated both the Latin teacher and the Housemaster who caned me. There was no way I was going to give either of them the satisfaction of 'winning'. So it was that I endured the pain of being hit every week. The dose increased from 2 strokes to 4 as the teachers - believing that they were caning me for my own good - increased the level of 'encouragement'. But the pain of regular caning was never enough to counter the internal pain of giving in to my oppressors.

The punishment continued until my father, learning after some months what was happening, wisely sent me across the seas to another school. He never asked why I did not surrender to the primitive 'encouragement' that I had been enduring. I guess he knew me well enough to know!

4.3
THE MIND THAT LOOKS AFTER ITSELF

We often use adjectives like 'self-centred' or 'self-seeking' in a judgmental way to describe someone who seems more concerned about their own needs than we think they should be. The reality is that all of our mental processes are designed to serve our own internal notions of well-being, or to help us avoid perceived distress. Because each individual is an internal control system (a bit like a thermostat), we are each designed to maximise our own internal experience of pleasure and to minimise threat or whatever we feel as pain.

What provides pleasure is very personal - just ask a random group of people what will constitute 'the ideal weekend'. Similarly, we all have a rather idiosyncratic perception of pain. As a former marathon runner who loved to push my body to the limits, I know that most people will regard that 'pleasure' as rather eccentric. But then I don't really understand the fascination of social media or a love of gardening!

I want to make a strong point here. Everyone is genetically programmed to look after themselves. It's important for leaders to be wide-eyed and pragmatic about that reality. Expecting anything else is to be doomed to disappointed. However, I am not saying that this self-orientation is a bad thing – it's simply how it is. It's the way that the brain and its attendant mind function.

So, having accepted that everyone seeks their own version of pleasure and avoids whatever they personally regard as painful, let's examine the operations of the mind in more detail and start to draw out some of the significance of these processes.

4.4
MOTIVATION

Each of the three functions of the mind:
- Perceiving
- Deciding (by comparing)
- Behaving

has distinctive features that explain both the diversity and the individuality of behaviour. The different ways we come to see things, the motives for our actions and the actions themselves are inter-related and play a particular role in our becoming the person who we present to the world.

The working of the mind may best be understood by taking these three functions separately to begin with, starting with the deciding or comparing process that is the source of our motives and which generates our behaviours.

Central to how this 'comparing' process works is that we attempt to match our perceptions of the world as closely as possible with the way that we would like the world to be.
This idea of 'the way we want things to be' means that we always have internal references[10] to which we are comparing our present experience.

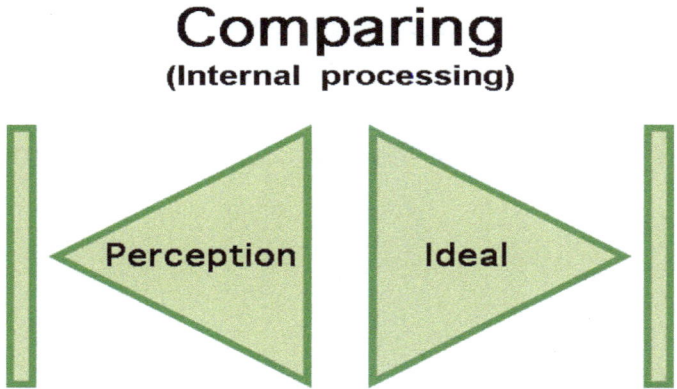

Comparing
(Internal processing)

We create these internal references ourselves. From the time of our birth, we store impressions of our experiences. When the experience is particularly pleasurable or meaningful, we naturally want to repeat that pleasure. In this way, these representations of our 'ideal' experience become the references against which we compare our present perceptions. These ideals are the experiences we seek.

This collection of internal representations or 'wants' thus forms the 'ideal' against which we compare what is happening to us right now. William Glasser[11] described these collections of pleasurable experiences as mental 'pictures' which are stored in our 'Quality World'. He likened our internal processing to a comparison between what we are presently experiencing and the 'wants' in our Quality World.

We can illustrate the comparison like this:

In this way, the common driver of our behaviours is the juxtaposition of what we are experiencing and one or more of the 'wants' in our Quality World: this is the internal motivation that we all experience. Motivation is always internal because it is our individual and personal 'wants' that we are trying to match with experience.

Glasser usually described these 'wants' as pictures, and the Quality World as like a personal picture album of our preferences. But our preferences are not just pictures (visual images). They can be beliefs, sensations or ideas; they can relate to people, places, activities and objects. They may be consciously recalled or be largely subconscious: subliminal fragments on the edge of awareness.

When we compare our perceptions of how things are to the 'wants' in our Quality World, there will either be a match between the two, or there will be a difference.

When there is a match - when we are actually experiencing Quality in the moment - we are content. However, when our perceptions don't match our ideal, then we experience frustration. This sense of frustration sends a signal to our behavioural system to do something to change what we are perceiving: to improve it, to bring our present experience closer to the ideal.

As Glasser did, we can use the analogy of a set of old-fashioned weighing scales where what we perceive to be happening is on one side of these scales, and what we want is on the other.[12]

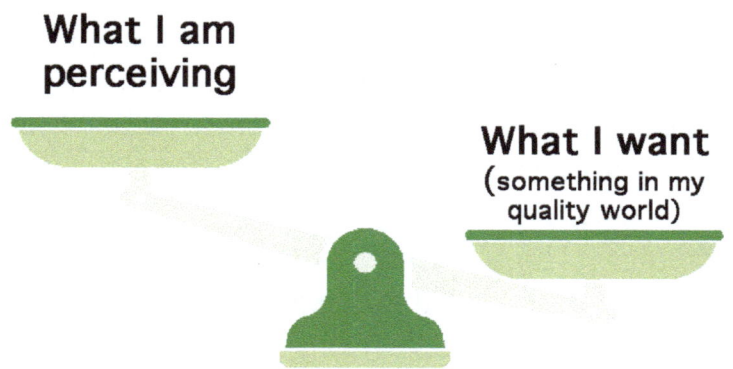

As an internal control system, we are always behaving to keep the scales in balance, with what we want on one side weighed against what we are presently perceiving on the other.

In this way our 'wants' (our personal collection of Quality World conceptions) provide a navigation chart for the conduct of our lives. Because they are the representations of how we would like the world to be, they explain how we choose our behaviours.

Most of us have many such attractors, so we don't always have the same Quality pictures or preferences in mind. We have many representations of what is ideal in our head and they are mostly context dependent. Even the enduring features of our ideal world (such as our family or our favourite leisure pursuit) are only sometimes the 'want' that we place on the scales.

4.5
CHOOSING THE WANT THAT WE PAY ATTENTION TO

Critical for our self-management is understanding that we have a choice about which of our representations of Quality to put on the scales at any time. For example, when I am tired and at the office late into the evening, I can choose what to weigh against the hours I am spending to complete a project. If I weigh what I am doing against the vivid quality picture of going home and relaxing with a glass of wine with my wife, I will very likely feel dissatisfied that I am working so late. If on the other hand, I weigh my late hours of effort against the satisfaction I know I will feel when the project is competed I will probably feel quite differently. Probably, instead of feeling disgruntled I will have a sense of accomplishment.

In both these cases, I will still be working late - on the same project. My perception of what I am actually doing will not change. However, what makes a difference to whether I feel relatively content or rather unhappy is what I am comparing with what I am experiencing.

Knowing and appreciating that we have some choice about what 'pictures' to weigh against our present experience is vital for self-management. Choosing to manage ourselves by eliciting 'wants' that encourage effort and self-efficacy makes such a difference to our actions and to our attitudes.

Applying this insight, I realise that I will have many choices as a leader about what to put on the scales when something goes wrong. If a colleague miscalculates or does not get a work assignment done on time, I can weigh their error against the inconvenience that results - <u>or</u> against the opportunity for me to address the development of that person. If I focus on the immediate inconvenience and delay in achieving a business goal I will be tempted to blame the team member or take over the job myself. Conversely, I could recognise the mistake as an opportunity to coach and mentor. Once again the circumstances are the same – something did not work out. However, what I choose to weigh against this makes a big difference to how I am likely to deal with the situation.

Notice that this is not just a matter of how we see things (perception). It is directly related to the want that we put on the scales to weigh against our perceptions. If we choose an unhelpful 'want' we can easily sabotage our long-term intent by making a decision that will damage rather than support our leadership effectiveness. Sometimes people think that they have little choice about the internal representation they are using to weigh against the perceived 'reality'. However, the truth is that this is one of the many choices that we can make in managing our mind.

Some of these choices are easy – for example, we know it's not sensible to carry a Quality picture of fillet steak into a vegan restaurant. That would be to guarantee disappointment! Other choices are far more difficult and require us to be highly disciplined about our decision over which internal reference to weigh against the circumstances. Perhaps the most critical of these Quality conceptions is our choice of our own identity as a leader.

Leadership falters when we seem to put our own personal self-interest, short-term success or desire to dominate on the scales. The ideal we have for ourselves as a leader brings very different approaches to the role. If our ideal of our self as leader is of a supervisor who has all the answers; who is superior to the other people on the team; whose position gives them the right to be obeyed, then it will probably follow that we will manage the staff in a controlling way. That approach to leadership is not uncommon but will always have negative consequences for relationships and trust.

If on the other hand, our reference for ourselves as an ideal leader includes responsibility for building capacity and creating a culture of energetic commitment; if we are mindful that success is a team effort; if we ever conscious of our dependence on the work of the staff, then it is likely that we will have different priorities. We are more likely to be encouraging and inspirational in the way we work with the team. Choosing the way we envisage the role of leader creates a very important reference point in our quality world.

One more thing about our Quality World. The pictures in it (the wants against which we compare reality) are not static, even though they don't change easily. As we learn and mature with the experience of life, we construct new representations of whatever becomes our personal versions of Quality.

Our childish wants are replaced by more adult quality experiences. However, we do have difficulty taking well-established pictures out of our Ideal world. Once we have a person, idea or experience in our personal ideal space, we don't easily forget them or reject them - unless we can replace them with newer and more satisfying pictures. This is significant for leadership. We can easily be misled by out-of-date quality pictures, or by wants that are appropriate in other life roles but which do not support our leadership endeavours.

4.6
NEEDS – THE UNSEEN GENERATORS OF OUR MOTIVES

Although we have many of them, there is a pattern to our stored Quality pictures. **Each is a way of satisfying one or more of our genetic needs.** When we refer to pleasurable experiences, the source of that pleasure is that a need is being satisfied. It's probably more accurate to say that we seek need-satisfaction rather than pleasure: the pleasure comes from the internal reward we experience when a need is satisfied.

Once controversial when proposed by Maslow[12] and later by Glasser, the existence of genetic human needs is now widely accepted. They explain so much about us. Different theorists and researchers name the needs somewhat differently, but the similarities between their appellations are more significant than the differences they identify.

According to Glasser[13] there are five needs. We will use his appellations to introduce them. One of these is clearly biological in origin with its seat in the more primitive parts of the brain. This is the **survival** need. Safety, security and certainty keep this need satisfied. The need for survival and pain-avoidance, and its positive equivalents (comfort, safety and procreation) are located in the most primitive brain area – the brain stem.

The other needs are cognitive. They are related to the most evolved structures of the brain: the cortex and particularly the pre-frontal cortex (the brain's directive system). We experience these cognitive needs as:

- A need for **Power** (to feel powerful, important, significant, worthy, competent and in control, mastery);
- A need for **Belonging** (to be connected to and close to another or others, to love and be loved, to be included and accepted);
- A need for **Autonomy** (to be self-determining, free to make our own choices, to act willingly);
- The need for **Fun and Learning**. Almost everyone agrees that the need to learn is fundamental to being human. At birth, compared to other creatures we are relatively helpless, but our capacity to learn enables us to exponentially expand the range and capacity of our behaviours. What is distinctive about Glasser's conception is that he believes that the chemical reward (Dopamine) that supports human learning is so strongly associated with the feelings of enjoyment that we get

from playing and having fun that it is appropriate to group learning and enjoyment together.

Other authorities in this field name the needs slightly differently. In the list above and in the diagram below I have included the names given to the needs by such diverse writers as Edward Deci[16], Daniel Pink [17] and Abraham Maslow[18].

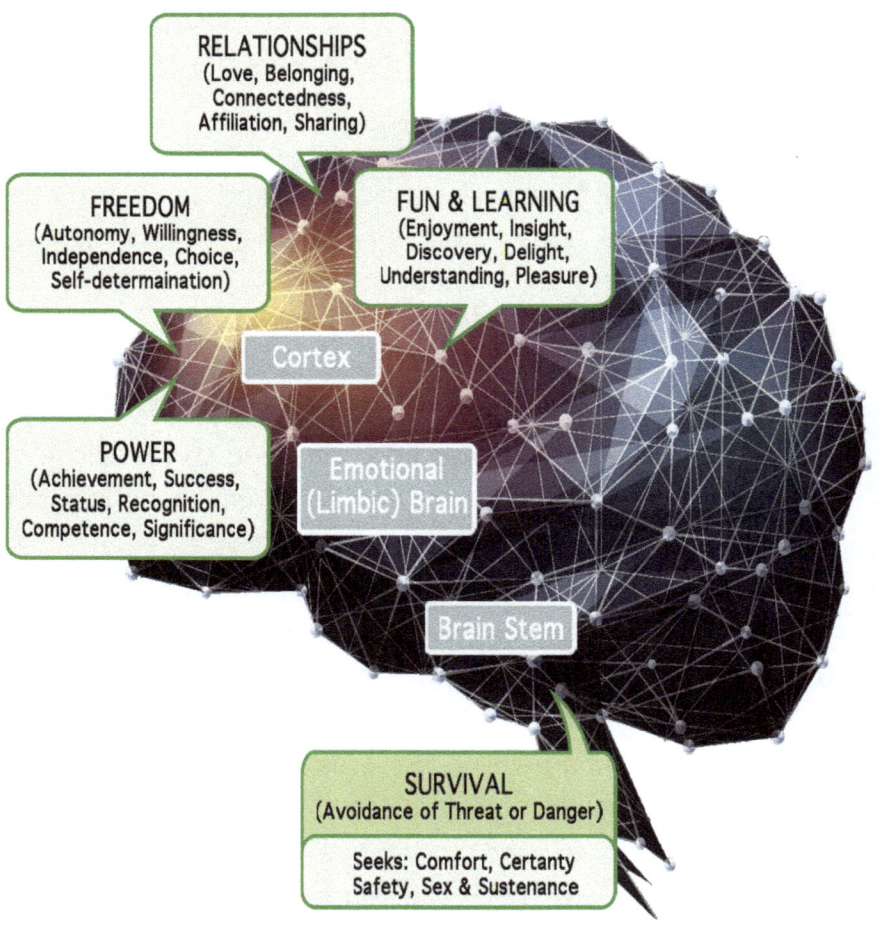

No matter how we name the needs, all of the specialists in this field agree that it is the unrelenting imperative of the human mind to find ways to satisfy these biological and cognitive drivers. It is this that gives our wants (our Quality World pictures) such a powerful place in creating our behaviours.

I like to believe that, in addition to Glasser's four cognitive needs, we all have a need for **meaning**: to believe that there is a purpose to our lives and our work. Victor Frankl[19], who titled his reflections on the experience in the WWII death camps as *'Man's Search for Meaning',* argued that with a sense of purpose humans can endure great hardship, but without meaning they easily surrender. Frankl founded his logotherapy practices on the belief that we all strive for meaning in order to be psychologically well. For me, the critical evidence is the negative experience. Those who find life and work to be meaningless are usually deeply discontent. The malaise associated with meaningless activity is universally recognised as a debilitating experience. The harmful result of a need unsatisfied points strongly to its existence!

Although many people argue that this restless search for meaning simply shows that it is a derivative of the other needs (rather than a separate need), I have always found it pragmatic to think of meaning as if it were a need. It points to one of the great precepts of leadership which is to structure work and the workplace in ways that point to the meaning and purpose of the business. If work is meaningful; if the leader has a noble purpose that their team buys into, then the quality of work and commitment always seems to accelerate.

4.7
THE NEED FOR AUTONOMY

I think it's important to point to the compelling research that shows that one of the needs has a particular significance for leaders: the need for autonomy.

Self-Determination Theory, the theory developed and researched by Edward L. Deci[20], suggests that this need is crucial to work behaviour. We will return to look at this again more fully in later chapters.

In summary, it seems that individuals at work do seem to have a powerful need to be the author of their own behaviours; to be willing participants; to buy-in and have a sense of choice about their endeavours. Without willingness, there is often little sense of wellbeing. Perceiving oneself as self-determined affects the way in which the other needs are satisfied. Personal achievement and self-concept (Power) almost pre-suppose autonomy. Learning (and the enjoyment that accompanies it) does not occur when we are following someone else's script. Further, almost everyone finds it difficult to establish a fulfilling relationship with a person who is insisting that they must do as they are told!

4.8
AVOIDING PAIN

What is described in the paragraphs above explains one kind of motivation. For most of us most of the time it is our primary motivation. It is what we might call our 'moving towards' motivation - the urge to repeat or approximate need-satisfying experiences. Our internal 'wants' are always urging us towards positive experience.

It's important to notice however that there is another kind of motivation which is inspired by self-protection, and which we might describe as 'moving away from' motivation. The survival need is strongly involved with this kind of motivation.

The mind's decision-making process works in a similar way with both kinds of motivation, but there is a difference. When we are behaving to satisfy a need we are trying to get closer to our ideal. When we are influenced by the second kind of motivation, we are in avoidance mode: we are attempting to distance ourselves from something we don't want. When we are 'moving away from', we are comparing our perceptions that something is dangerous or is threatening to our ideal of safety and wellbeing. We fear events or people that we perceive as likely to obstruct the satisfaction of our needs, cause us pain or distress, or even threaten our health and survival.

With this kind of motivation, the mental process still involves comparing our wants (how we think things should be) with our perception of what is happening. However, in these circumstances, the behaviour generated is intended to steer us away from internal pain by avoiding the threat, rather than by increasing need-satisfaction *per se*. Clearly, the need that is responsible for the avoidance of physical pain (which is just one example of 'away from' motivation) is the survival need. But it goes further than physical survival.

In writing about this kind of response, David Rock[21] draws on the new wisdom of neuroscience to hypothesise that this kind of motivation is strongly associated with the survival need in the social context. He contends that, because humans are social animals, this avoidance response can be related to social survival.

Rock suggests that the survival response is triggered by any perceived threat to our:
- **Status** (the way we are regarded; our importance);
- **Certainty** (our sense that the world is predictable and our clarity about what is occurring);
- **Autonomy** (our free-will or ability to exert personal control over events and their outcomes);
- **Relatedness** (our connectedness with other people and the security of these relationships);
- **Fairness** (our feelings about whether we are treated justly and equitably).

An important feature of the 'moving away from' type of motivation as described by David Rock, is that it often overrides our positive attempts to improve the quality of our lives. Until the threat is perceived as having passed, people tend to focus on survival (both physical and social) before turning back to satisfying their cognitive needs. In the diagram below (which draws on David Rock's S.C.A.R.F. hypothesis and Glasser's conception of needs), I have tried to illustrate the way in which threat 'hi-jacks' positive motivation.

Social Threats v's Psychological Rewards
An interpretation by 'FutureShape Consulting' of the relationship between Social Threat [SCARF © David Rock] and the Cognitive Needs [Glasser]

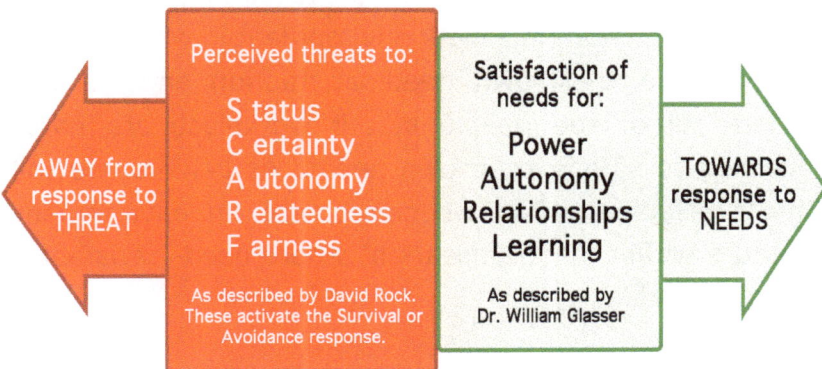

The way in which we tend to deal with threat before addressing need satisfaction is probably why Maslow[22] positioned the survival need at the base of his 'Hierarchy of Needs'. Although there are certainly times when our cognitive needs do override our survival need (for example, some people enjoy reckless fun with no thought of the dangers involved; others commit suicide through loneliness or feelings of failure), nevertheless, most of us are too unsettled to focus on what we really want when we are distracted or distressed by our perception of threat.

4.9

IMPLICATIONS FOR LEADERS

I will refer in subsequent chapters to many of the implications of the way in which motivation works in ourselves and in our colleagues. However, let's note for now that leadership effectiveness often depends on the way the motivation process is understood, specifically:

1) Leaders who understand that they don't need to motivate anyone, because everyone is motivated internally, will tend to focus on creating a work environment in which their staff can pursue their own need-satisfaction and meaningful goals. All of the people in our workplace are naturally inclined to satisfy their own needs. As leaders, we will be most effective when we can create an environment (a culture within the organisation) where need-satisfaction is encouraged.

   It isn't the leader's job to take responsibility for satisfying the needs of their staff – that is something each individual can only do for themselves.
   However, it is the leader's responsibility to work with their colleagues in such a way that each of them can experience personal achievement, reasonable levels of autonomy, positive relationships at work, and thus have opportunities for meaningful learning. This is need-supportive leadership!

2) Leaders who are sensitive to the disengaging effects that can follow from perceptions of threat will appreciate the importance of anticipating and limiting the way their actions may trigger the threat response.

   Using David Rock's S.C.A.R.F responses as a guide, but re-framing them to the positive, we can:
   - Work respectfully with our staff and encourage personal achievement and the growth of capability (Status);

- Create a sense of certainty about the direction, values and beliefs that are embedded in the vision and purpose of the organisation (Certainty);
- Allow every opportunity for team members to stamp their personal style and creativity on the way they do their work: in other words, let them 'do things in their own way' (Autonomy);
- Work actively to create and nurture trust, inclusion and supportive relationships within the organisation (Relatedness);
- Treat all of their staff, whatever their role, even-handedly and justly, always providing thoughtfully expressed reasons for decisions that affect people (Fairness).

3) Knowing that everyone has a unique Quality World, leaders who want to maximise their influence will know that listening to and learning about what excites and energises both individuals and groups within their staff will pay dividends.

4) We can't **make** our colleagues do anything! Attempts to coerce or control our staff will result in either resistance or disengagement. Knowing this, effective leaders understand that the more connections they can make between their own conceptions of Quality and those of their team members, the more influence they are likely to exercise.

Chapter Five

The Input Processes of the Mind

"Thought creates our world and then says: I didn't do it!"

David Bohm (Quantum Physicist)[1]

5.1
The Deceptive Practice of Perception

We have noted that the generator of human behaviour is a comparison - a process through which we weigh up what we want against our present perceptions of what **is**. Because of this, knowing how the perceiving process works is also critical to our understanding and appreciation of the people we lead.

Perception is the input dimension of the complex brain processes that create the totality of human behaviour.

Perceiving

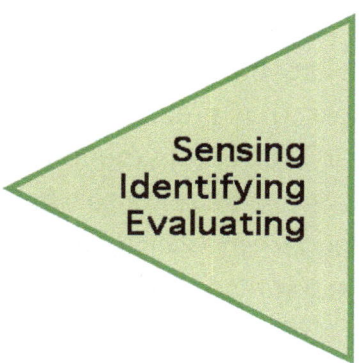

Although our brain creates the illusion that we are observers of an accurate representation of the world as it is, we know from the science of perception that our five senses simply receive packets of energy that are then translated into the electrical and chemical activity of our brain. This activity then expresses itself as mental phenomena.

In our 'mind's eye' what we seem to see, feel, hear, smell and taste appear to have real substance, even though each is simply a cognitive translation of our sensing.

Even our five senses are somewhat unreliable sources of information because we can only attend to a small amount of the information that we get from them. The current scientific estimate is that we can pay attention to somewhere between 4 and 9 bits of sensory information at once[2]. Even when we switch our attention rapidly, we are missing far more than we can possibly take in.

Whatever sensory data does reach our attention is then interpreted through the lens of all our pre-existing knowledge, experience, memories and schema. None of the information we are receiving from our senses can possibly come to us without being coded by what has gone before. It's this internal interpretation process that creates the lenses through which we then view our current experiences. We know this instinctively: we provide knowledge to a child in a very different way from the manner in which we present that same information to an adult. We know that the lenses of their experience are very different.

5.2
THE KNOWLEDGE 'LENS' CREATES BELIEFS

We don't store all the knowledge that comes to us through experience. We recall and re-access the information that seems significant to us. Some knowledge appears especially important because it seems to help us to understand and manage our lives successfully in ways that satisfy our needs. We adopt this special knowledge as truth about how the world works. This kind of trusted perception we call our beliefs.

Sometimes we treat beliefs as though they embody truths that transcend their usefulness and apply them in situations where they do not lead to what's best for us. This is especially harmful when they are beliefs which are limiting us in any way. The proper test of beliefs is whether or not they are useful. Their truth value is based on their utility, not on some transcendent absolute.

This may seem somewhat heretical to you. Many of us are not used to this way of thinking about our beliefs, but let's think about how they are formed. A series of experiences convinces us that some actions or circumstances help us, and that others hurt us. We adopt a belief on the basis of very few experiences (sometimes only one) and then we generalise this to apply to the totality of our experience, in order to simplify our decision-making in the future. Unfortunately, once we have adopted a belief, we tend to ignore counterexamples, or manipulate our interpretation of events so that they fit our belief. Through these processes of generalisation, deletion and distortion[3], we cling to beliefs that do not (or no longer) support our effectiveness as human beings.

Let me give just one example - (I am sure that you will think of many more). Some years ago, I got to know an experienced draftsman. When this very busy and successful man was introduced to computer-assisted graphic design, he found it difficult to connect this new process with the sophisticated hand-drawing skills he had mastered. He was introduced to it in a rather intimidating way. His manager told him: "This is the future and you have to master it!" He was taught in a perfunctory manner by a far younger person who had little patience with older men who had not yet converted to technology solutions.

The draftsman was confused and became fearful of this new approach and clung to a former belief: "A computer will never be able to do this work as well as a skilled professional like myself." He also adopted a new belief: "I will never be able to use this CAD stuff." These two un-useful beliefs underpinned his approach to the changing world of his work and eventually sabotaged his career.

Limiting beliefs such as the ones described above are a blight on the lives and careers of countless people who have learned to think that their beliefs are immutable, rather than to evaluate their beliefs reflectively. Within a space of a few days, I heard quite experienced executives illustrate their unhelpful beliefs by saying:

- "I can't do difficult conversations – I always make things even worse."
- "It's no use expecting me to inspire my team. That's just not me."
- "I inherited a negative staff culture and I won't be able to change it until some key people leave."

Notice that these statements embody beliefs that are 'true' for them at that moment, but the beliefs are self-fulfilling. Their strategies will be influenced by their belief. Recognising that the belief is not useful to their success, while at the same time adopting a useful one will open up a new world of strategic effectives – for example: "I can learn how to be more effective when I need to have a difficult conversation."

5.3
THE VALUES LENS

Stored in our mind are all of the values that we have developed to the present point in our lives, as well as all of our experiences of pleasure and pain. Remember that these are self-created internal references. With these we attach meaning and merit to the sensory data we are receiving.

When we value something, we are giving it Quality status. We allocate positive value to experiences, ideas and behaviours that are need-satisfying. We also allocate negative values to whatever we believe will harm us. We form values in a similar way to the way in which we form beliefs and they have a comparable pervasive effect on every aspect of our experience.

The result of this active process of perceiving is that nothing passes through the portals of our perception untouched: all our perceptions are shaped and influenced by what is already in our brain, as illustrated below:

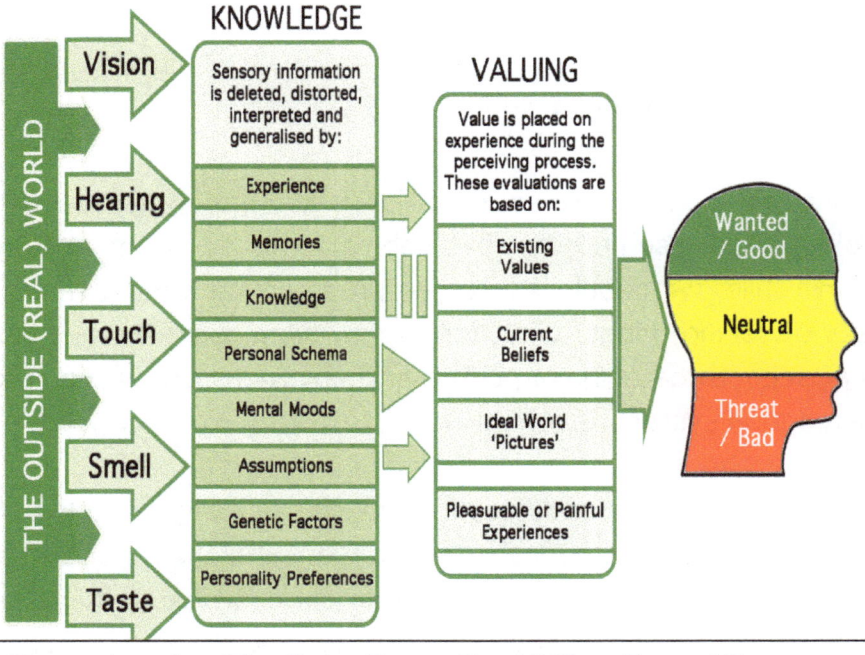

Diagram based on 'The Choice Theory Chart' William Glasser MD

In short, we perceive the world as it is interpreted by us, not as it is. Our own perceived world, which is a drastically simplified version of the 'real world', is acquired through the limited lenses we create as we learn and grow.

This means that our personal perceptions are somewhat unique: no one else has accumulated the identical experience and values with which to interpret the world. In essence, what we create through our perceptual system is not the world as it is, but the map of the world that we have created.

Although it always seems to us that we know the truth of things, that our perceptions are 'right', this sense of certainty is a self-deception[4].

5.4
IMPLICATIONS FOR LEADERS

When as leaders we seek to influence and persuade our colleagues of something that seems to us to be manifestly worthwhile, we should always be prepared for their different way of seeing things. What for us may seem exciting or useful may seem threatening or pointless when processed through the perceptual system of others.

Understanding these differences in the perceived worlds of individuals is often critical to effective leadership. Ineffective leaders tend to cling bombastically to their own perceptions of how things are and discount the opinions, beliefs and values of others as simply wrong. Effective leaders adopt the advice of

Stephen Covey[5]: *"Seek first to understand and then to be understood."*

Similarly, a powerful metaphor formulated by Alfred Korzybski[6] reminds us that: *"The map is not the territory."* Our conceptions of actuality spring from our mental representation of the realities that bombard our senses. There are always differences between perception and reality, and each of us has our own version, our own map of reality. But from the wisdom of the NLP community comes a truism that mirrors Covey's advice: *'To influence another person, first learn to understand their map of the world in order to draw them towards your own.'*

Once again there are remarkably clear leadership messages to be taken from understanding the uniqueness of individual perceptions:

1) Learning to understand our own maps of the world and the way that they were formed is important for our own self-management. If we are unaware of the preferences and assumptions that influence our thinking, it is so much harder to manage ourselves. Without insight into the distinctive beliefs that underpin the way we go about things, and the experiences that generated them, it's very easy to behave unreflectively.

2) When we don't appreciate the distinctive nature of our own perception, we are in danger of communicating our own blinkered view of reality as if it were 'the truth.' We can then fail to grasp the danger that this may impede rapport and even generate resistance.

3) When we understand and manage ourselves, we can regulate our own attention in order to be open and attentive to the different perceptions of others. From this understanding and appreciation of the way our colleagues see things, we can:
    - continually update our own maps so that our depiction of reality is as current and up to date as we can make it. There is nothing more damaging to a leader's effectiveness than acting from a personal but inexact conception of what is really going on;
    - begin to identify and draw upon the connections between our map of the world and the maps of our staff: this is the foundation of powerful influence.

Chapter 6

Behaving

"From birth to our death, all we can do is behave. Every behaviour is total: it consists of acting, thinking, feeling and physiology."

William Glasser MD[1]

6.1 Behaving: The output process.

Behaving is the output function of our mental processing. Once our comparing process has weighed up the difference between what is happening and what we want, the only way to close the gap between the two is to generate a behaviour that will improve the situation.

Behaving

When we refer to 'behaving' we almost always think of actions. However, one of Dr. Glasser's important contributions to the psychology of behaviour was to point out that:

- There are 4 dimensions of human behaviour: Acting, Thinking, Feeling and Physiology (body response).
- All the dimensions are aligned with each other, i.e. we always have a total behaviour, not 4 different behaviours.
- The acting element of behaviour and the related physiology are visible.
- Thinking and feeling are less visible (except as revealed through our actions and physiology).
- We have relatively direct control over our own acting and thinking, but only indirect command of our emotions and physiology.

6.2
THE METAPHOR OF THE CAR

Glasser's useful metaphor for total behaviour can be represented by the 4 wheels of a Car². We can steer with our acting and thinking behaviours (the front wheels), but our feelings and physiology are like the back wheels of the car: they are strong energisers of behaviour; they provide us with important information, but they depend for their direction on the front wheels.

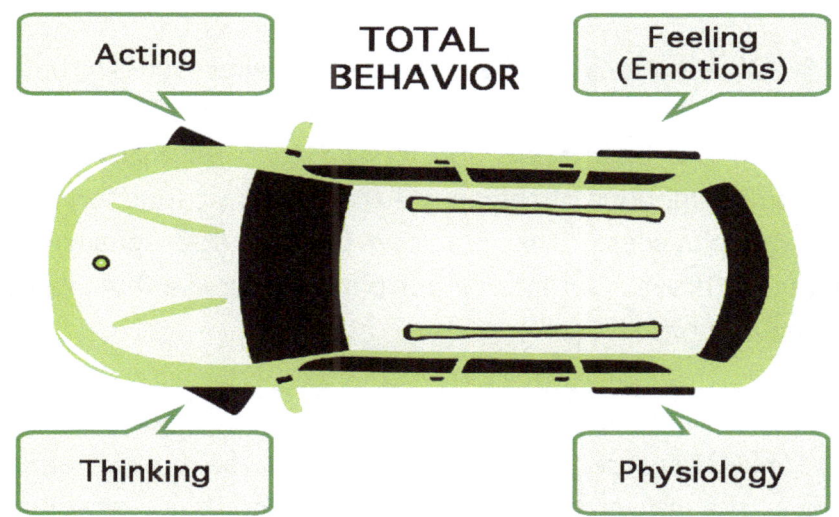

Let's look at critical ways in which the car metaphor can help us understand and manage our own mental functions:

- When we appreciate that any particular behavioural 'state' or total behaviour is associated with the component (wheel) that initiates or dominates it, then we realise that changing from an unhelpful state to a more effective one is possible by choosing to activate a different behavioural dimension or 'wheel'.

- Because our back wheels can only be controlled indirectly (by changing our acting and thinking), we can easily get stuck in a 'back wheels' behaviour. Negative or painful feelings, and the associated physiology, tend to be experienced as overwhelming - as if they have taken over our state. It can certainly feel like that. Unfortunately, many people don't know, or do not appreciate, that it is only by changing their acting or thinking that they will experience different emotions.

The brain's emotional centre is the limbic brain which is situated close to the most primitive part of our brain. This 'old brain' is located in the brain stem and it takes care of many of the autonomic functions of the mind – the ones that function apart from consciousness. This primitive brain is also sensitive to danger or threat – threats to our physical survival but also to our social survival.

When this old brain senses danger, it instantly activates the emotional brain. Because it is closest to the brain stem, it receives the information first. The developed brain - especially the pre-frontal cortex, which is the rational director of our behaviour - is further from the brain stem than the limbic brain, so signals passed through our nervous system take longer to reach the rational brain. Thus, an emotional reaction to a situation that is perceived as harmful or threatening is felt before the cognitive brain has a chance to interpret it, or to calm the sense of fear. This explains why we seem to 'react' to some situations with anger or fear with no opportunity to choose another response. It's a built-for-purpose structure for survival. Primitive humankind needed to trigger the 'flight or fight' response immediately to maximise the chance of survival, and we are still designed the same way. We can't avoid this non-rational reaction when confronted or menaced. However, it's important for leaders to **manage** their response.

6.3
MANAGING OUR BEHAVIOURS

Knowing how behaviour works, we *can* manage it. In the grip of an unhelpful emotion, we can learn to change our feelings and physiology by taking action or by deliberately managing our thoughts. Actions such as deep breathing, walking fast or any physical exertion inevitably alter our physiological state. We can also direct our thinking in helpful ways – for example, by attending to aspects of the situation that we can control, or by concentrating on the impression that the 'ideal me' would like to make at that moment.

Managing our behaviour like this is not easy! It takes practice and self-discipline. But however difficult, this is the level of self-regulation necessary for those wanting to enhance their *Leader-Mind.* The people whom we lead and work with (those with whom we must gain influence and develop trust) can't see our intentions. They see and hear our behaviours. From what they perceive, they draw conclusions: about whether we are trustworthy; whether we are consistent; whether we mean what we say. Learning to manage our emotions, challenging as that may be, is the key to presenting a consistent, reliable and responsible face to the people whom we wish to inspire and engage.

One frequent problem that we all encounter as we try to develop and demonstrate this level of mind-management is that we often have to override existing patterns of behaviour.

6.4
Habits

All our behaviour is our best attempt at the time to get more of what we want - or to avoid what we don't want (or a complex mixture of both!) When a behaviour is successful (at least for a while) we tend to automate it (i.e. learn it) so that we can activate that behaviour easily. This learning or habituation process is mostly beneficial. It means that we don't have to invent a behaviour every time we need one. However, sometimes it can be a problem because under pressure it's easier to call on a learned behaviour than to 'invent' a new one. When that happens, we sometimes call on a behaviour that has been useful in the past, but which is not the best choice in the present situation.

I want to emphasise this point. All our automated behaviours were created at some time in our lives to serve us. That does not mean that the same behaviour will be useful or productive in the context of leadership. For example, children learn behaviours like 'throwing a tantrum' - and persist with this behaviour if their parents decide it's easier to let the child get his or her way than to be firm. There are lots of behaviours like this that we learn when we are children (e.g. sulking, lying and blaming other people). We learn them if they worked at the time. They are behaviours that may seem to have served us well as children. They are not attractive or connecting behaviours when they emerge in us as adults.

Nobody is impressed when the boss flies into a rage or 'spits the dummy'!

I once sat in on a teleconference where a very senior leader performed an adult version of the tantrum for 20 expletive-filled minutes. I think that all of the dozen or so executives who were on the other end of his rage understood that he was frustrated, but his expression of it was childish. He managed himself very badly. As a result, he lost the respect of the senior team on whom he depended. Because they now saw this element of unpredictability and lack of self-control in his behaviour, their trust in him diminished.

Now you might think that when a behaviour is unproductive, we would quickly unlearn it and look for an alternative – and indeed effective people often do this. However, as Daniel Kahneman[3] points out, our less-impulsive thinking behaviours (what he describes as our slower mode of thinking) are quite often used to justify these un-useful behaviours by blaming others or complaining about the circumstances. Replacing a well-practised behaviour with an unfamiliar one involves accepting the feelings of temporary incompetence or awkwardness.

It takes a significant measure of self-discipline to always take responsibility for your own behaviour rather that justifying or excusing it. But, without this discipline, there is no learning and no improvement.

All of life is an opportunity to keep learning new effective behaviours, and to recognise and replace the behaviours that were well-learned in the past, but which may harm us now. Acquiring the adaptability to abandon well-practised actions when they don't work for us is a feature of developing *LeaderMind*.

6.5
LEADERSHIP BEHAVIOURS

The leadership implications of this function of the mind include the following:

1. We arrive at this present point in our lives armed with a repertoire of learned behaviours, some of them influenced by our personality preferences and cultural heritage, but most adopted to deal with the circumstances of our unfolding life. The question for us as leaders is: Do we want to rely on what we have learned and automated so far – or keep on learning? It is almost certain that what got us to this point will not serve us well in a future that will inevitably be different.

   As leaders, choosing to rely on the repertoire of behaviours that we have already acquired, or to extend our range, is an ever-present challenge. The evidence of human achievement shows that the more behaviours we have on call and the greater our store of behavioural possibilities, the more adaptable we become, and hence the more likely we are to succeed.

2. As leaders we have a choice: to learn from experience or simply to repeat our experiences. It's very tempting to do the latter. Our mental processes are organised in a way that

is designed to register the differences between the effects of our behaviour and what we intended – and then to seek an even more effective behaviour. But this only happens if we take responsibility for the outcomes of our behaviour.

If we blame others, or the circumstances, or if we justify what we did when things don't work out, we don't learn anything. But it takes moral courage and rugged self-evaluation to ask ourselves what else we could have done: what we could have done better. Of course, there may have been difficult circumstances, or other people may have acted irresponsibly, but none of this prevents us from learning. If we don't achieve the outcome we had hoped for, there is almost always something different that we could have done, and which might have been more productive.

3. Habitual reflective practice is the tool which helps us truly learn from our experiences. This is not simply rumination or perseveration. Almost all of us do that two o'clock-in-the-morning routine when we replay the events of the day and their consequences. Self-evaluative reflective practice is very different from this: it is a rigorous application of a self-coaching process. It addresses the questions:
    - What happened?
    - What did I want?
    - What's the difference?
    - What else could I have done?
    - When and how will I change the way I behave in the future?

4. We can coach ourselves, as well as others, using coaching questions that include the process of self-

evaluation (as illustrated above). Coaching both self and others is a critical skill for leaders. It is a way of 'disrupting' our un-useful learned behaviours and replacing them with more productive ones.

5. Leaders learn most productively when they are prepared to take risks. It's easy to say, but much harder to do. When we take risks, we abandon the safe harbour of our habitual and familiar way of doing things and venture into the unknown; and because we are leaders - working in the public eye of our organisation or team - we have to do this very visibly. We go from doing something that we know we do well (but which is not working) to attempting something new. By definition, this will look and seem awkward. It can threaten our sense of competence and our confidence in our credibility with others. The hard truth though is this: without this risk, there can be no change, and without change our capability cannot grow.

6.6
THE WORK OF THE MIND (A SUMMARY)

"The more we are able to create space between stimulus and reaction, the more control we will have over our emotional lives."

Chade Meng Tan[23]

Let's summarize what we have learned about the way in which the human mind works to generate behaviour:

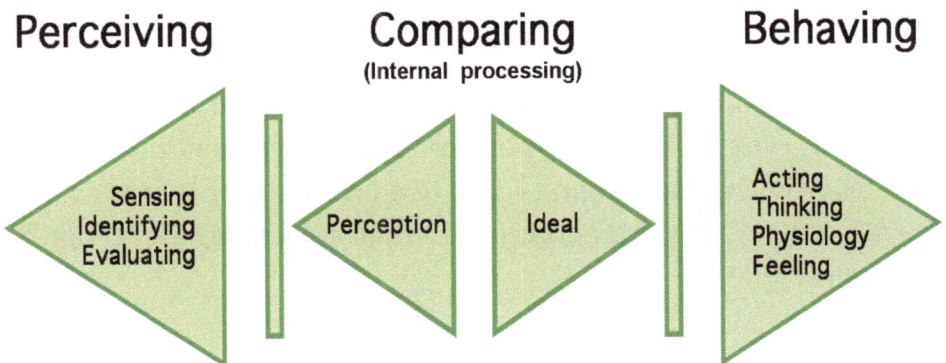

The inputs into our behaviour do include the context in which we live and work and the behaviour of others. However, it is our perception of these, and the results of the choices we subsequently make - not the contingent events and actions around us - that produce our responses.

Our perceptions are always compared to the 'want' (our Quality World picture) which is relevant to the situation. When there is a gap between what we want and what we are perceiving, we will then generate a behaviour which will be our best attempt to close the gap between what is actually happening and how we would like it to be. Sometimes this may be a goal-oriented behaviour to increase our sense of control over events; sometimes an avoidance behaviour to distance us from apparent threat to our wellbeing.

When we do not have a behaviour that will improve the situation, our mind's creative capacity is designed to look for something else that we can do. However, we can override this aptitude. Instead of looking for a solution; a new and more useful behaviour we can blame others or make excuses in order to avoid the hard work of identifying and learning a new behaviour.

Mindful leaders choose to address the problems of their work and their lives by taking responsibility. Knowing that whatever the situation we can separate ourselves from a simple reaction, calm our emotions and adopt useful thinking and acting to find solutions.

SECTION THREE

CHAPTER SEVEN

THE TOOLS OF LEADERSHIP EFFECTIVENESS

"Leaders are not born. They are made. They are made just like everything else through hard work. That's the price we have to pay to achieve anything."

Vince Lombardi[1]

Chapters Seven to Nine form the core of this book: they describe three critical mind-management tools that are needed by those who want to acquire *Leader-Mind*.

These three disciplines are:

- Knowing what you most want (Chapter Seven).
- Accepting responsibility (Chapter Eight).
- Rigorously self-evaluating your own behaviour (Chapter Nine).

Chapter SEVEN

Knowing what you want

"If we are prepared to work for them, many things we want are within reach – but not everything. We have to make choices. We have to be willing to pay the price!"

Glen Gerreyn [1]

7.1
Knowing what you want

Many years ago, I sat at the dinner table of a friend and listened as Dr. William Glasser, the guest of honour at our gathering, talked informally about his work.

There were many questions for Dr. Glasser as you can imagine, but one stuck in my mind. One of the guests asked him if he had a simple way of introducing the ideas of Choice Theory and Reality Therapy to people who were not familiar with his work.

"Sure" he replied: **"Everything I teach is about knowing what you want and how to get it."**

As this whole book is about knowing what you want as a leader, and knowing how to achieve it, Dr. Glasser's words provide a suitable maxim to introduce the core of this book. If learning to acquire and use *Leader-Mind* is about anything it is about knowing what we want and how to achieve it.

The three chapters of Section Two present three key cognitive habits that will help you to acquire the practices of *Leader-Mind:* to remain focused on what you want as a leader and work towards achieving it. As you will discover, they are such powerful instruments that, if you allow them to, they will help you to manage your life as well as your leadership.

These three cognitive disciplines are:
1. **Knowing and remaining focused on what you most want.**
2. **Accepting responsibility.**
3. **Rigorously self-evaluating and calibrating your behaviour.**

This section is mostly devoted to just these three practices because they are crucial to the mind-management that is needed for leadership effectiveness.

Of course, these three self-disciplines don't stand alone. One or more of them is embedded in almost all of the other processes and practices that are presented in the remaining sections of the book. Without these tools, managing your own mind can be elusive and confusing. With these three practices you can increase your control of the thought and actions that will lead to the best outcomes.

7.2
WHAT THE EFFECTIVE LEADER WANTS

If we refer to our effectiveness formula, it will help us to keep the focus on what, as leaders, we really want.

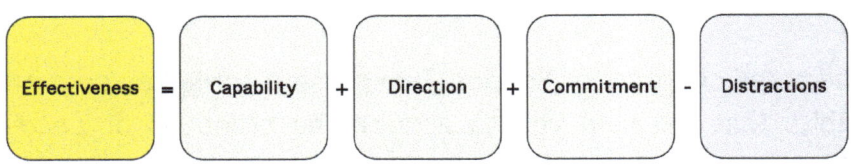

If our main 'want' is to do our job as well as we can so that our people and our business will thrive, then that goal is our priority. Our focus will be building capacity in and around ourselves – remember the paradox of power - in ways that maximise the commitment and engagement of our team members and provide them with clear direction.

Of course, multiple other urgencies and distractions bombard our attention. It's easy to become distracted; and the biggest distraction is to pursue short-term or secondary goals.

As Scott Peck[2] observes, the mind-management tool that we all know as 'delaying gratification' is learned by almost all of us in childhood but is all too often ignored when we become adults.

So it is that short-term goals can easily distract us from our primary aim. The urgent can supplant the important. Proving ourselves right in some trivial matter, but in a way that erodes our long-term influence, is all too common. Failing to invest in capacity-building because other things seem to have higher priority at the time, and then bemoaning the lack of capability around us, is a tragedy so commonplace that it is unremarkable.

The three mind-management tools that follow in this section are the instruments that sustain the journey to achieving *Leader-Mind*.

7.3
KNOWING WHAT YOU REALLY WANT MATTERS!

As a long-time fan of Yogi Berra[3] quotes, one of my favourites is:

"If you don't know where you are going, you might wind up someplace else."

I suspect that it is the fate of many leaders to end up 'someplace else'. It's not that any of them intends to spend time and energy on activity which will take them in unhelpful directions, it's just that it all too easily happens. Un-managed, our minds, faced with the complexities of a leader's work, can lead us down many false turnings and into unwanted corners.

Let's expand a little on our knowledge of behaviours from Section Two. You will recall that once we have created a behaviour that is effective in matching our perception with one of our internal references or 'Quality' pictures, we tend to repeat it and learn it. Consequently, one of the significant results of learning a behaviour is that with repetition we are then able to automate it – to call on it again without conscious thought whenever the behaviour is needed. The behaviour becomes a familiar pattern, a habit.

This unconscious use of learned behaviours is of real benefit to humans as a species. It means that we can perform many complex behaviours without having to think about what we are doing. Very useful - but also potentially problematic! The unconscious nature of our well-learned behaviours easily leads us awry. It's easy to summon an automated behaviour when it's actually nearly-but-not-quite fit for purpose.

Does this sound a bit abstract? Let's use a specific example. A friend of mine, who we will call Lucas, really wanted to build a strong team around himself ('want' or Internal reference 1). However, he himself had learned to value attention to detail (Internal reference 2). He had also adopted the practice of keeping the most complex and important tasks for himself to make sure that they were done correctly. "If you want something done properly, do it yourself" was something taught to him by an early mentor and he often repeated this mantra (Internal reference 3).

Because he had not yet developed the practices of reflection and mind- management, Lucas did not appreciate that there was significant conflict between his Quality pictures. As a result, whenever the 'team' was faced with a challenging situation, he would either take over completely ("If you want it done well, do it yourself"), or micro-manage the work of the responsible team member to make sure the details were right. The members of his team felt that he did not trust or value them and were sceptical about him and uncommitted to his agenda – which he often complained about. In this way, two of his well-established internal references and the behaviours that he had learned to associate with them, continually undermined his efforts to build the strong team he really wanted. And, of course, his actions created a self-defeating outcome: i.e. because he did not trust anyone else to do things as well as he could, he denied them the opportunity to learn how.

Another brief example: Grace was a fiercely competitive person in her personal life and brought this to her work. As a former triathlon champion, her competitiveness and her belief in herself had served her well. As a leader, she was hard-driving and often made impulsive 'let's go for it' decisions. She recognised this and knew that she needed a strong, trusted lieutenant who would give her thoughtful analytic advice as a complement to her more intuitive preferences. However, when her second-in-command Andrew (who preferred the reflective and systematic approach that Grace needed for balance) offered an opinion, Grace's need to 'win' resulted in her defending and justifying her impulsive tendencies. If she felt she was 'losing' she would taunt Andrew with being too cautious and deliberate. Andrew soon learned that Grace's tongue was sharp and her opinions hurtful. He decided it was less painful for him to stifle his misgivings about a proposed course of action, with the result that Grace continued to make impulsive and unreflective decisions – to the detriment of her own career.

As you can see from these examples, the actions we are tempted to take out of habit, or from the pursuit of a want that 'in the moment' seems important, are often not helpful. Without the discipline of attending to what we really want, it's easy to be distracted by our habitual thinking or by less important wants. Too often, a superficial want will lead us to a different 'someplace else' from the outcome that is most important to us.

7.4
WHY IS THE REAL WANT NOT OBVIOUS?

There are two related reasons why we often act instinctively or chase after the first 'want' that pops into our heads:

1. One difficulty is created by the multitude of pictures that we have stored in our 'Quality World'. As we live our lives, most of us have multiple need-satisfying experiences: occasions when what we want is matched with gratification of a need. Some of these Quality pictures are more important to us than others. If we were always at our most reflective, and with our thought processes in complete control, we would always think through the consequences of our actions and choose to pursue our most important 'want'. Unfortunately, as we have seen in the examples above, the needs are often in conflict. For example, our need to have good relationships is often in conflict with our needs for power and freedom. We all want both, but sometimes we exercise our power in ways that are likely to alienate us from the people we most need to influence - a common dilemma!

2. A further problem is that it's rare for our mind to present us with the conflicting wants of the moment in any kind of order or hierarchy. We have to do that through her own self-management. This is hard thinking work, which is why we

need a process to support our own mind-management: a process for sorting through the 'wants' our cognition presents to us so that we can pursue the ones that are most important to our happiness and effectiveness. We can't satisfy all of our needs all of the time and, when needs conflict, we have to make difficult choices.

3. Unfortunately, we need to apply a significant degree of discipline in our reflective practices, because the type of thinking we apply to sort out our priorities does not always work in the way we expect.

In 'Thinking Fast and Slow', Daniel Kahneman[4] explains that our fast, intuitive thinking – the thinking that we use most of the time to make swift, agile decisions about the world - often errs. Kahneman describes this as our 'Type 1' thinking, and our reliance on that thinking mode often leads us a little astray. No worries though. As Kahneman tells us, we have our 'Type 2' slower, more reflective thinking to help us out – except that too often it doesn't!

Certainly, our reflective 'Type 2' thinking is better at supplying reasons and pondering more deeply than our more intuitive 'Type 1' processing – but it can work in two different ways. Our slower thinking mode can spend itself on either justifying the results of our 'Type 1' thinking - or challenging them. It's quite common for it to choose the road of self-justification!

If you are at all observant of your leader colleagues, you will have noticed this from time to time. A great deal of energy is often spent on giving reasons for, or explaining, a poor (un-reflective) initial decision which is leading to unintended unproductive consequences.

This could be an opportunity for 'Type 2' thinking to kick in using analytic, reflective mode to review the decision. In many cases, what actually happens is that our slower mode of thinking is used to protect the ego and develop all sorts of arcane justifications of the original bad decision – a tribute to the inherent creativity of our cognitive processing. Despite this rationalisation, the initial decision may sabotage the leader's noblest intentions **and** the purpose of the organisation. In all the huffing and puffing however, the problem created by the initial intuitive conclusion gets lost in obfuscation. Proving that we got it right (even when we got it wrong) is often preferred to backing down and accepting that there may have been a better way.

7.5
BEWARE THE INTRUSION OF THE 'DON'T WANT'!

As we saw in Section Two, there are two reasons why we are often more conscious of what we don't want that what we do want:

1. We are always comparing our present perception to our 'ideal' or Quality picture. We feel frustration when our perception and the present 'want' don't match. Because of that internal signal, that feeling of frustration, we notice when things are **not** as we would like them to be much more strongly that when our present perceptions and our ideal are a match.
2. Our survival need reminds us all the time about the existence of threat. Our primitive brain, located in the

brain stem, does its job very efficiently. So well does it look out for possible pain that it ensures we alert very easily to both physical and social threats. If this self-consciousness of potential harm is not managed very well, it's easy for anxiety and self-protective behaviour to dominate our thinking.

The antidote to the distortion that the 'don't want' creates in our thinking is to manage our minds to focus on the associated positive want.

Consider the following: every want is associated with a need through a Quality picture that we have created. The 'don't want' is generated by the frustration (or potential frustration) of that need. The mental discipline of focusing on what we want instead of what we do not want is powerful and effective. My colleague Judy Hatswell[5] describes this process as 'Flipping', which is a very evocative and useful description of the process.

To illustrate how this works, look at the table below. The 'frustrations' in each horizontal band are presented in the left column as they relate to each of Glasser's 5 needs. On the right are the 'flipped' wants relevant to each expression of frustration.

When we become conscious of a 'don't want' (a negative perception that we are trying to avoid) it's important that we 'flip', so as to deliberately pay attention to the positive. This is valuable both for ourselves and for the people we lead.

Negative perception (frustration)	Positive value (the want)
Need: Relatedness Lonely, left out, disconnected, unwanted, isolated, alone, ignored, in conflict.	Connected, involved, included, in harmony, considered, liked, loved, befriended.
Need: Power/Achievement Helpless, incompetent, not respected, fragile, frustrated, unsure, not capable, unsuccessful, uncertain, unvalued.	Confident, composed, capable, respected, valued, competent, powerful, successful, important, thriving, effective, skilled.
Need: Autonomy Frustrated, constrained, limited, coerced, forced, obstructed, restricted, reliant.	Liberated, willing, in control, independent, autonomous, free, self-sufficient.
Need: Fun and Learning Bored, weary of, uninterested, finding dull or tedious, indifferent, , disengaged.	Learning, enjoying, stimulated, interested, entertained, challenged, having fun.
Need: Survival Fearful, threatened, frightened, apprehensive, intimidated, bullied, alarmed, insecure, pessimistic, sick.	Safe, secure, confident, protected, trusting, healthy, optimistic, hopeful, self-assured, calm, brave.

Flipping to the positive want has three benefits: it leads to clarity, utility and vitality.

- As leaders, we are always trying to be clear about what we want for our team or organisation. This gives our colleagues clear direction. In contrast, when we express

a negative perception (a 'don't want') the people whom we lead are ushered into a world of conjecture. They have to guess what it is that we actually want – creating a potential for misunderstanding and confusion.
- We also want to take the course of action that is most useful to us in achieving our business and team goals. Avoiding a 'don't want' leads to defensive behaviour: we spend time and effort protecting ourselves and the business from something. It's almost always more useful to strive for what we want than to spend energy and effort insulating ourselves from what we fear or want to avoid.
- The energy cost of avoiding threat rather than pursuing a positive objective is considerable. When people are motivated by anxiety, they never work with the same energy or effectiveness as when they are pursuing a positive outcome. The perception of threat triggers, from our limbic brain, the release of chemicals that impede our clarity of thought and our creative capacity. In contrast, with the anticipation of positive achievement the limbic brain releases Dopamine: the neurotransmitter that energises us.

7.6
EFFECTIVE LEADERSHIP IS ALWAYS ON THE SCALES!

When Dr. Glasser generalised about the nature of his work by defining it as 'knowing what you want and how to get it', the crux of his definition is in the first four words: _knowing what you want_.

Knowing what we want in order to be successful leaders, and keeping this as our main priority, is essential. Whatever other thoughts and feelings bubble to the surface of our consciousness, leadership effectiveness is our prime concern.

As Glasser[6] did, we can again use the analogy of a set of old-fashioned weighing scales where what we perceive to be happening is on one side of these scales, and what we want is on the other. As we manage our own thinking, leadership effectiveness will always be on the 'want' side of the scale.

Putting effective leadership consistently on our scales is not as easy as it sounds. As we have already noted, as human beings we want many things, so we have many depictions of how to satisfy our needs stored away in our 'Quality World'. Often these 'wants' conflict with each other. We can have ideals about ourselves deserving respect, winning, dominating; about fairness, accountability, our ideas being 'right'; about our 'position' being important. If we have these measures on our scales, we will behave to achieve them - especially because many of these 'wants' have strong feelings attached to them.

There is nothing wrong per se with having these wants in our 'Quality World'. These values - and the feelings that go with them - are part of our persona. Wanting these things, and the self-confidence that comes with attaining them, have been useful to us at some time in the past. But when we are choosing the *Leader-Mind* pathway, we have made a commitment to a choice that always takes precedence. We have decided that leading others productively; building capacity and effectiveness; enabling our team to thrive; is always our prime Quality picture.

This sounds challenging! I can hear you asking: "Does this mean that it should always come first?" The answer is 'yes', but it's not actually that difficult. It's just one choice. The challenge is sticking to it.

By way of illustration, let me tell you about a conversation I had many years ago with the great Emil Zatopek[7], winner of the 5,000 metres, 10,000 metres and marathon at the Helsinki Olympic Games. Zatopek's running style was not pretty, but his training methods - based on intense and sustained effort - were legendary.

I asked the great man about the mental discipline involved in training strenuously every day for so many years. He answered like this:
"I made one decision: to train very hard every day. One decision is easy. Other athletes make it difficult. They choose every day: 'Shall I train today?'; 'How hard should I train today?'
So many decisions – new ones every day. And always the question of making the right decision! Now that is hard!

I choose the easy way. One decision. Train as hard as I can every day."

Acquiring *Leader-Mind* is the same kind of discipline. Make one decision – to put your leadership effectiveness first, every time there is something to put on the scales: each time you are weighing up what to do. Following the *Leader-Mind* way means always putting on the scales the image of ourselves as leading in the manner that will draw out the best in others; that will give them clear direction and encourage their commitment.

7.7
DELAYING GRATIFICATION

One of the other complications of making a commitment to always choosing to place leadership effectiveness on our scales is that the pay-off takes some time to emerge.

As we learn and extend our capacity, we all acquire the ability to delay gratification. None of us would have worked through the self-discipline of extended study or practice in order to achieve our qualifications and skills without it. Delaying the satisfaction of short term wants and needs is one of the most critical mind management tools for anyone who wants to be successful. It's the mainspring of effective parenting; of responsible financial management; of training in any skill. It is the discipline required of everyone who wants to succeed. Yet, even though this discipline is commonplace, and is developed by most children quite early in their lives, it's often forgotten or ignored in the rush of living and leading.

One reason why we can often choose immediate rather than delayed gratification arises from the brain's perplexing difficulty in differentiating between the 'urgent' and the 'important'. Another comes from the multiple demands on the leader's time. A third challenge is our tendency to take on the easier tasks first and procrastinate over those that require considerable reflective attention. One or another of these three creates a predictable outcome: whatever is at the front of mind at any moment is easier to deal with than what is most important.

So it is that we can easily 'tick off' the easy tasks that cross our desks and feel satisfied by the illusion that we are accomplishing something – only to find that nothing important has been achieved!

As practitioners of *Leader-Mind* we will notice that time spent understanding and coaching a colleague; talking with the people who perform small but vital roles in our organisation; taking the time to teach and nurture a skill; letting someone know that you have noticed their efforts are all slow-growth activities with a pay-off in the future. They 'feed forward'.

Building trust and capacity is often a long labour with a distant reward: it is payment into the savings bank of fruitful relationships. The benefit may be far in the future. But when the time comes for the leader to make a withdrawal from this reservoir of thoughtfully-nurtured credence and ability, then the emotional currency will be in the bank. All the deposits will have been worth it.

CHAPTER EIGHT

RESPONSIBILITY.

"The road to power is taking responsibility. It doesn't matter whose fault it is that something is broken. It's your responsibility to fix it. When it's your life, your happiness, your success, it's your responsibility and your responsibility alone!"

Will Smith[1]

8.1
ACCEPTING RESPONSIBILITY

If knowing what you want is the first key discipline of the *Leader-Minded*, then accepting responsibility is the undeniable second.

If the only person we can control is our own self - and it is - then taking responsibility means that we can always have some measure of control. We can't control anybody else, and we are not responsible for what they do. We may not be able to control the consequences of an event or the outcomes that follow from the behaviours of others. However, what we *can* control are our own thoughts and actions.

This discipline is not complicated, and it is related to the first (knowing what we want). Whenever there is a challenge to be faced or an issue to be dealt with, we ask ourselves and our team: "What can we do to retrieve or improve the situation?" When an unexpected set-back occurs, we ask ourselves: "How can I or the team exploit these circumstances?" And always, of course, the pursuit of effectiveness for ourselves and our enterprise is 'on the scales'.

Scott Peck[2] wrote: *"We cannot solve life's problems except by solving them. ...and we must accept responsibility for a problem before we can solve it. We cannot solve a problem by saying 'It's not my problem'. We cannot solve a problem by hoping that someone else will solve it for us. We can solve a problem only when we say, 'This is my problem and it's up to me to solve it'."*

Whether the events and circumstances that ebb and flow in our lives and work are good or unfavourable, we can only influence them through the behaviour of the one person we can control – ourselves. We will not always be able to make things right or improve every circumstance, but we can always do what we can do – which is to harness our thinking and our actions - so that they manage our emotions and physiological state. With this self-control, whatever problem or situation confronts us we will be able to deal with in the most productive way possible.

8.2
THE ALTERNATIVE: OUT OF CONTROL!

When I discuss the discipline of taking responsibility with the leaders who attend my workshops, someone often asks: "Why should we take responsibility for a problem that we did not create?" The answer is this: we are not taking responsibility for creating the problem - unless we actually did create it - in which case we should certainly own up to it! What we are doing by taking responsibility is exerting whatever influence we can on what happens next. There is no point in dwelling on the past: it's what we have learned from that experience and what we do or say next that counts.

If each of us is the only person we can control, and we **don't** take responsibility for managing ourselves to improve or rectify the situation, we are choosing loss of control. That's a logical but painful reality.

Not taking responsibility has two effects: one on the leader personally, and the other on the people they lead. When we don't take responsibility, we feel helpless. When a situation or problem confronts us or our organisation, if we are telling ourselves that there is nothing we can do, then we are impotent. We can of course spend unproductive time and energy identifying, accusing and convicting whoever is to blame - or we can shift the responsibility to someone else in the hope that they can and will fix the problem. Both those actions require us to surrender our personal power and accept that we are incapable of taking useful action. Surrendering to incapacity is anathema to leadership effectiveness!

THE LEADER-MIND EQUATION

As Stephen Karpman[3] so cogently illustrated with the 'Drama Triangle', the only alternative to accepting responsibility for one's own circumstances, actions and options is to take one or more of the three positions on the triangle: i.e. blame someone, expect someone else to fix things, or adopt the perspective of victim. All of these are positions of surrender. If we spend time and mental energy blaming others; or complaining about circumstances; or making excuses for our own mistakes, then we get locked in our own private version of Karpman's Triangle.

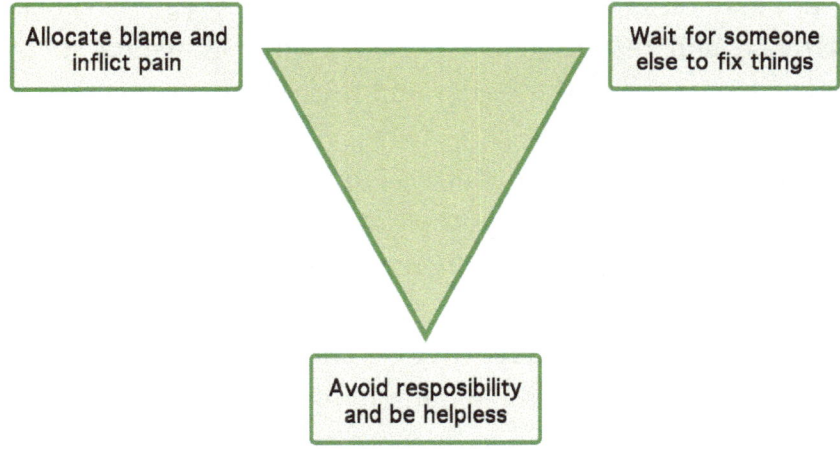

As the model shows, all the behaviours in the triangle are symptoms of an inability to deal with circumstances competently, and the only way out of this blame/complain cycle is to take responsibility: to do whatever we can (however little) to make things better. Keeping in mind that we are always attempting to enhance the effectiveness of our leadership and the capability of our team, there is always *something* that we can do.

8.3
THE CONSEQUENCES OF EVADING RESPONSIBILITY

Our 'common-sense' thinking can easily take us down the dead end called 'finding out whose fault it is'. From the usual perspective, it does seem right that whoever creates a problem should be responsible for solving it, but there is not even a slim measure of effectiveness in pursing this avenue of action. Apart from the effort and time consumed (usually without addressing the problem situation), blaming also generates defensiveness, resistance and resentment – none of which is useful to the relationship between the leader and their staff.

The even greater consequence of avoiding responsibility by 'finding out who is at fault' is the culture it creates. Remember: we are positively motivated when we are attempting to satisfy a need. We are motivated in a different way when we are avoiding pain. If making sure that we are not blamed is the kind of motivation that is common among our team members, our business will be one in which everyone watches his or her own back and makes sure that they avoid making mistakes. This is not the culture of learning that is so important to growing capability. The key to building capacity is for everyone to know with certainty that improvements - in individuals or in the organisation – are not possible without learning: and learning always involves making mistakes to begin with.

8.4
THE TWO CHOICES:

If we follow the argument above, the leader has two alternative ways in which to respond when something has not worked out as intended:

"Who made the mistake?"

or

"That didn't work out. What will we do next?" What did we learn?

Of course, the leader who is genuinely attempting to build capacity will not neglect their own learning. As Edgar Schein observed[4], the leader's own attitude to learning has a powerful effect on the creation of a learning culture. The leader who knows that they must set an example through their own willingness to learn and change will, of necessity, become the chief mistake-maker – a very visible sign that learning is being attempted. This gives considerable impetus to the establishment of a culture of development and growth. Schein also noted rather sadly, that a leader's unwillingness to learn is often the chief inhibitor of learning across the organisation!

Some years ago, I observed the astonishing change created in a large education district when the leader changed. The outgoing leader prided himself on 'kicking butt' when people were underperforming. He actively pursued individuals who had made any error or did not achieve to his expectation. The result was that people hid their mistakes, fabricated performance results and spent a great deal of energy making sure that they protected themselves.

The new Director took a very different approach. She owned up to her own limitations and freely discussed with her senior colleagues ways in which she could improve her own performance. When a mistake was made, she initiated positive debriefing to determine what could be learned for the future. She encouraged experimentation and enterprise. She championed reflective practice and coaching to help people learn and improve. They did!

The key to the self-improvement, and the organisational development that comes with learning is a radical dedication to truth: an unwillingness to make or settle for excuses; to use every mis-take as an opportunity to learn and build capacity. That's why the third discipline in this section is self-evaluation: the ability to manage one's mind in order to review and re-calibrate your own behaviour.

Chapter Nine

Self-Evaluation

"There is no failure, only feedback."

Tad James[1]

9.1
No failure. Only feedback!

This is one of the empirical pre-suppositions of the set of communication and self-development procedures known as NLP (*Neuro-Linguistic Programming*). Put very simply, NLP explores the inter-play of language and the brain, and ways to use that language to access the resources of the mind.

This particular pre-supposition is a healthy one with which to approach self-evaluation. We self-evaluate in order to provide ourselves with reflective feedback. From that reflective feedback we can generate new behaviours: behaviours that will move us closer to what we really want.

In the fields of science and technology, 'no failure, only feedback' are important operating principles. No innovation is the result of a single attempt. We can't expect to learn and improve the products of our actions without experiencing 'failure'.

The problem that we humans face, especially in the field of leadership, is that we are emotional creatures - and those emotions can make us quite tender in the face of awkwardness and the fear of appearing less than accomplished. As noted a few pages back, we have an unhelpful tendency to justify our less-than-ideal actions, rather than subject them to thoughtful scrutiny as a way of learning how to do better.

Developing the habit of self-evaluation brings with it the helpful pre-supposition that everything we can do can be improved: that 'failure' is conducive to learning. Thus, adopting a process for comparing your goal with the results achieved so far (remember that this is the way the mind works), is the key to continuous improvement.

9.2
THE PROCEDURES FOR SELF ENHANCEMENT

The third of our key disciplines, the 'mind management' tool that is the essence of 'LeaderMind' is derived from Dr William Glasser's 'Reality Therapy'[2]. This procedure, which is powerfully therapeutic in the clinical setting, is also the most potent self-evaluation and coaching practice I have encountered.

Because I am not a therapist, simply a leader who was seeking a process to manage his own thinking, I found the 'therapy' part of the name problematic at first, until I realised that these procedures are wonderful coaching and self-coaching tools[3].

These days - in the spirit of Dr. Glasser's simple explanation at our dinner gathering in 1996 - I often describe these procedures (in their several guises) as 'working out what I want and how to get it'.

Essentially, the 3 elements of these procedures for tuning the mind to achieve what you want are:
1. Strive for clarity about what you really want: your most important priorities[3];
2. **Evaluate everything you have done or considered so far (to achieve the outcome you want);**
3. Consider further options (and their likely consequences) and commit to at least one of these.

I will describe the procedures in the way I use them to self-evaluate: to manage my own cognition (this is my 'self-coaching' if you like). In the capabilities section that you will find in Section Four of the book, I describe how you can employ the same process to coach another person.

9.3
Step 1 - Achieving Clarity

"Clarity is what a person's mind is always endeavouring to return to."

Jamie Smart[4]

While I agree with Jamie, achieving clarity is an endeavour that is greatly assisted by using a systematic process. Without a procedure to harness the mind's natural search for comprehension, it's easy for our thoughts to get stuck at superficial levels.

The questioning process described below takes us systematically to our deeper levels of cognition.

In any circumstances when you feel that you need to get in touch with your most important 'want' – especially if your clarity of thought is threatened, or your thinking is clouded by emotion - ask yourself:

What do I want?
Whatever your answer to this follow up with:
What difference will it make if I achieve this?
Whatever your answer to this follow up with:
Why is this important to me?
Whatever your answer to this follow up with:
What will change for me, and the way I see myself, if I achieve this?

If you have responded to these four questions with reflective honesty, you will now be at the level of 'really want'. You will have greater clarity about whatever goal or preference you are pursuing.

Being clear about the 'really want' is the requisite starting point for working out how to achieve it. This is Step 1 in the process.

Before we move on, you might have noticed that there is an underlying structure to the four 'clarity' questions: -

The First question:	"What do you want?"	_ Asks for information.
The Second question:	"What difference will it make?"	_ Asks about what will change as a result (more information).
The Third Question:	"Why is it important?"	_ Is at the level of values - "Why is this change valuable?".
The Fourth Question:	"What will change for you? How will you see yourself?"	_ Is a question about identity – how we see ourselves.

This diagram illustrates the levels of this spiralling or clarifying process:

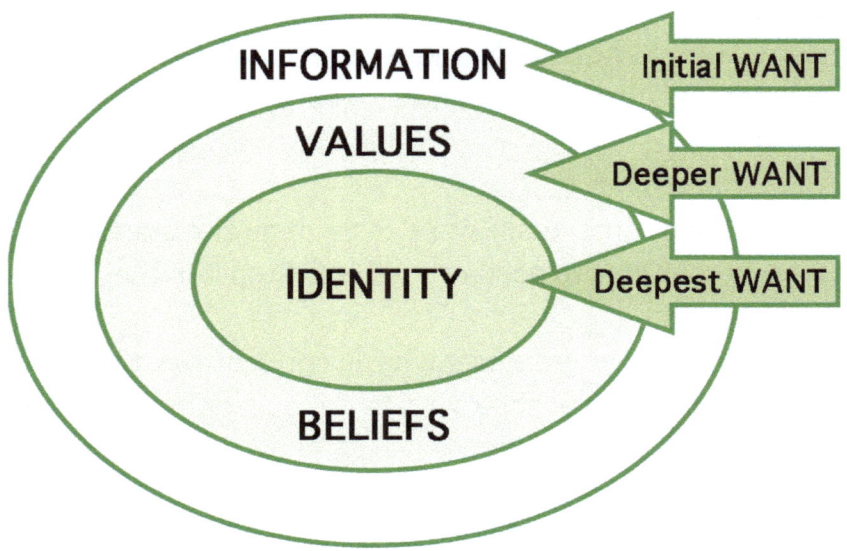

We first clarify what we want and the consequences or goal we are striving for (this is the information level). At the next level, we ask ourselves why what we want is important to us (the value level). At the deepest level, our reflective question is about the difference it will make to our sense of self and significance (the identity level).

9.4
STEP 2 – EVALUATING:
WILL WHAT I AM DOING GET ME WHAT I REALLY WANT?

The second step is the critical element in the process: self-evaluation. At this step, you ask yourself honestly about the effectiveness of your past and present actions. Did they help you to get to your 'really want', or can they can be improved? The questions are:

What have I been doing to get what I want?
and
Is it working?

These two simple questions are the archetype of the self-evaluation process that is critical to the power of these procedures.

These questions, and variations of them, cut to the heart of mind management.

Depending on the situation, you might be framing the self-evaluation questions in any of the following ways:
- Is what I have been doing taking me forward or backwards?
- Is doing what I have been doing improving my effectiveness or diminishing it?
- Have my actions been extending my influence or undermining it?
- Are my actions inspiring my colleagues or discouraging them?
- Has what I have been doing and saying built capacity?
- Will my people thrive if I continue to do what I have been doing?

However we present the self-evaluation to ourselves we are always in essence asking ourselves: "Is what I have been doing leading me to where I want to go?"

9.5
Step 3
Review your options - Make a choice - take action

The third step in the self-evaluation process is to review your options and implement whatever seems most likely to lead to success.

If, as the result of evaluating your actions, you realise that something that you are already doing is working well, you should very sensibly keep doing it (though you might also ask yourself if it could be improved.)

If the result of asking yourself the self-evaluation questions is a conclusion that your behaviours have not been working to achieve the outcomes you really want, then the message is clear: do something different! Choose new possibilities, new options. Take action. Then self-evaluate the results of your new actions.

Once you embark on the process of self-evaluation it becomes a cyclic practice. Because self-evaluation always results in **either** a re-commitment to what we are already doing, **or** a choice to take new action, there are always behaviours for us to try. These in turn are the subject of a new self-evaluation.

The result of using this procedure is that you will constantly be affirming or refining your practice; fine-tuning your behaviours - or choosing radically new ones. The goal is always to lead more effectively, achieve better outcomes, and build capacity around yourself.

In summary, the three steps of the self-evaluation process are:
1. Be clear about what you really want;
2. Evaluate everything you have done or considered so far (to achieve the outcome you want);
3. Consider further options (and their likely consequences) and commit to at least one of these.

SECTION FOUR

THE EFFECTIVENESS EQUATION

"He who would learn to fly one day must first learn to stand and walk and run and climb and dance; one cannot fly into flying."

Friedrich Nietzsche

Section Four of this book is about what a person who is focused on developing Leader-Mind will learn and do.

It provides the detail embedded in the equation:

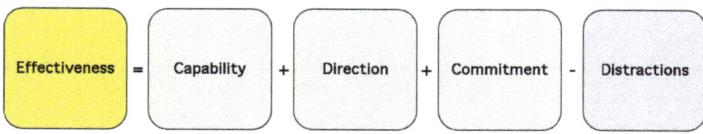

Chapter ten

A MANAGED MIND - THE PREREQUISITE CAPABILITY

"What we can or cannot do, what we consider possible or impossible, is rarely a function of our true capability. It is more likely a function of our beliefs about who we are."

Albert Camus[1]

10.1
THE EFFECTIVENESS EQUATION

The Leader-Mind equation for leadership effectiveness captures the significance of, and the relationships between, the four dynamic elements of a successful leader's work.

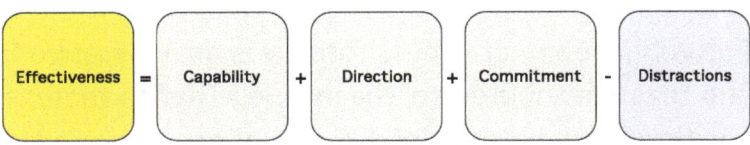

The formula applies both to the leader and to the people that he or she leads:

- Effective performance (in leadership or in the activity of the team) requires capability harnessed by clear direction and personal commitment. Effective practice deliberately evades the myriad distractions that are an inevitable part of a busy workplace.
- Effective leaders build capability and provide clear direction for their team. By creating a context that is rich in value and which enables the satisfaction of personal needs, they encourage effortful commitment.
- Effective leaders do everything they can to anticipate and manage potential distractions.

Each of these statements supports the others. When a leader is intent on effectiveness, staff capability is deliberately grown; the priorities and philosophy of the organisation are apparent to all; and trivia and 'busywork' are not allowed to detract from performance.

When there is a vibrant culture of effective learning in the team; when everyone understands where the business is going and why; when inessential activity and irrelevant detail are identified and separated from core business, then leadership in the organisation is effective.

The FutureShape effectiveness formula is an imperative for the present that contributes to the future. That's where a well-managed mind can be so helpful. It reminds us to do today what It would be so easy to put off until tomorrow.

It's a constant temptation to put off the challenging conversation that we know we should have now, or to put up with an ineffective system that is wasting everyone's time and energy because we believe it would be hard to fix. Managing our mental processes will lead us to managing out time and our systems so that they help us, not hinder us. None of us will be successful in the future unless we do our best to be effective today.

The formula asks us to consider: Whose capability can I build today? Where and how can I make our direction clearer (and to whom) today? What can I do at this moment to encourage commitment from my team members? What can I do today to eliminate (or ignore) potential distractions?

What we do today: the decisions we make today; the capacity we enhance today; the clarity we enhance today; the distractions we ignore or challenge today - these are the things we do to build tomorrow's effectiveness.

We can only work in the present. It is not that plans and dreams are unimportant; it's simply that they only become grounded when we take action in the present.

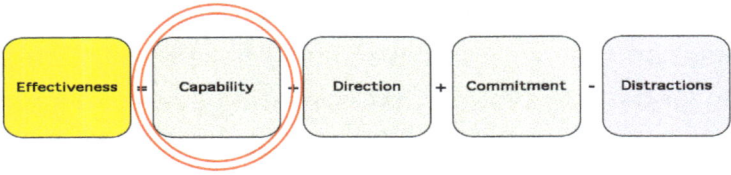

10.2
Capability:
Learnable Skills plus Excitement plus Practice

The idea that human capability is 'fixed' is a generalisation that serves us poorly. Although there is ample evidence that we are born with widely distributed proportions or raw ability in many spheres of performance, only a very few humans are so hampered by their brain's limitations that they cannot learn.

The assumption of static abilities flies in the face of recent evidence. If you still believe that capacity is fixed, then you have managed to sleep through all of the recent research findings about human learning, and neuroplasticity.

It doesn't matter which area of human aspiration we want to consider; the inescapable conclusion is that the one dimension in which humankind can choose to excel is learning. Anything we play seriously at; anything which we attempt and with which we persist in the face of initial failure; whatever we make a real effort to understand and practise: these things we will get better at.

This means that we can invest in the growth in capability of ourselves and our staff – the only condition being that in order to improve and develop the learner has to be a willing and committed investor in their own learning.

Norman Doidge[2], the doyen of brain plasticity literature, reminds us that:

"After the initial critical learning period of youth is over, the areas of the brain that need to be 'turned on' to allow enhanced, long lasting learning can be activated when something important, surprising, or novel occurs, or if we make the effort to pay close attention."

As leaders who use our knowledge of how minds work, we know we can't 'turn on' a colleague's mind: they must do that for themselves. But we can help to create the conditions in which they are most likely to flick that switch. If we create conditions that are safe and conducive to learning; if our colleagues know that what they learn and contribute is important; if we express our delight in new insight, then our colleagues are likely to 'switch on' for themselves.

10.3
Building Capacity

The biggest threat to our work in improving capability is that we will make judgements about a person's abilities and future performance (including our own) on the basis of past performance.

Talent is overrated. Early indications of aptitude are unreliable. Past performance is an ambivalent indicator of future behaviour.

It's certainly true that some people are early achievers, faster learners. They may indeed enjoy a genetic advantage that gives them a head start in their field of endeavour. But, as a former competitive runner, I could not help but notice how many wonderfully talented athletes did not rise to the top. The very top performers were often those with less initial 'ability' who had to work incredibly hard to succeed. Disciplined training, persistence in the face of adversity and a 'can-do' attitude took them past the field of natural talent.

It's the same with other fields. Of course, there are some gifted people who appreciate the endowment of their talent, apply themselves assiduously and take this talent to the top of their vocation. But the history of human success is crammed with individuals who started further back in the pack, who failed at school, or overcame the disadvantage of lesser creativity or physical prowess, but who went on to become the most celebrated heroes in their sphere.

It's our willingness as leaders to believe in and grow the capacity of the people we lead that encourages or inhibits the growth of capability around us. Some people don't see this; don't realise that their own attitude to the potential in others may be a critical factor in whether capability grows around us.

Many years ago, one of my colleagues, while deploring the mediocre performance of his own senior staff, commented on how 'lucky' I was to have many high-performing executive staff around me. I asked what he was doing to build capacity in his team. His answer "It's not worth the effort".

That was a self-fulfilling prophecy if I ever heard one! All I could suggest was that if he were to invest effort, he might be surprised at the change. For myself, I knew that to borrow a truism (derived from a quote usually attributed to the Golfer Gary Player[3]) 'the harder I worked to build capability around me, the luckier I became'.

"Discipline is the basic set of tools we require to solve life's problems ... the challenge lies not in the complexity of these tools but in the will to use them".

Scott Peck[4]

10.4
THE FOUR MIND-TOOLS OF CAPABILITY

If our challenge as leaders is to energise ourselves and our team members to build their capability through learning, then there are four disciplines, four mind-tools, that we can practise and teach.

The switches of human learning are often turned on or off by 4 mental activities that are in our control, although managing them sometimes takes considerable discipline.
These four cognitive disciplines are:

1. How we manage our emotions;
2. How we talk to ourselves;
3. How we direct our own mental imaging;
4. How we construct our own self-image (our self-concept).

The four are interrelated and affect each other. If we can improve our mastery of any one of these, it will improve our control over others.

Let's look at these briefly before turning to their application in three generic leadership capabilities.

10.5
Managing Emotions

As we have seen, behaviour has four inter-related dimensions. In Section 2, we used Bill Glasser's metaphor of the four wheels of the car to describe these. We are always thinking and acting, experiencing some kind of emotion and a corresponding physiological state. All behaviour is total: all four elements of our behaviour match each other - if one changes, so do the others.

Emotions are good at energising us (positively or negatively) and give us useful information. However, as far as possible, we should be cautious about inviting them into the driver's seat. The reason for this is that our emotions, and our physiology, can only be indirectly controlled.

It's comparatively easy to will a change of thought and action. If an act is within our physical capacity, we can learn to perform it. If we discipline our thinking, we can steer our thoughts away from distractions and into productive pathways – except that both of these can be hindered by emotion, and by the body states that accompany emotion.

As humans, we are an emotional species. The emotional centres in our brain are easily activated by perceptions of threat or pleasure. They then trigger a chemical response – the release of hormones into our system - that generates the phenomena we call feelings. Some feeling states are helpful and energising, others are distracting and debilitating.

If strong emotions 'take over' and create a physiological response, the emotion sometimes seems overwhelming because the chemical effects of the hormones released by our limbic system tend to cloud our thinking. Oxygen and glucose are drawn away from the pre-frontal cortex (our thinking centre) and flood our limbs readying us for flight or fight.

Despite the challenge, we <u>can</u> learn to manage our emotions. While we cannot change them directly, we can initiate thinking and actions that will effect a change. The conventional wisdom to take deep breaths or walk briskly are effective antidotes to the tension and elevated state of our physiology – they enable us to get onto the front wheels through action.

Similarly, if we self-manage well enough to direct our thoughts towards the positive; towards what we can accomplish and not to what is wrong, our thinking can take us off the back wheels and back into more effective control.

Another 'thinking' technique is to deliberately shift our attention into Third Perceptual Position. If we can describe what is happening to us, using our knowledge of how the mind works to describe the situation analytically, then the 'grip' of the emotion recedes immediately.

It's worthwhile to develop these habits of emotional control. They are a key dimension of the Emotional Intelligence[5] that a mind-managing leader must display.

Having acquired this control ourselves, we can encourage this capability in our colleagues. We can do this through modelling, by sharing the car metaphor and by introducing them to the tools of emotional self-management as a feature of our coaching and mentoring conversations.

10.6
Self-Talk

It's estimated that we talk to ourselves far more than we talk to anyone else. The undistracted mind tends to play a commentary that is almost unceasing. Disturbingly, I read recently about one piece of research which found that 80% of this self-talk is negative. That's frightening!

If we or our team members bombard our consciousness with messages that stop us learning or attempting things, then the associated thoughts (and feelings associated with them) act as a barrier to learning and growth.

Look at the table below and read the 'stopper' messages that are listed in the left-hand column. Then compare them with the positive alternative on the right:

- I might fail.
- I can succeed. If I try and do not succeed, I will have learned something.

- This is just like a past experience that was painful for me.
- This moment is not the past; it's a new opportunity.

- I don't have the ability or energy to succeed.
- I can accomplish whatever I apply myself to.

- I can think of so many ways this could go wrong.
- I will focus on all of the ways this could succeed and what that might mean for me.

- I feel helpless and overwhelmed.
- I am capable and I am confident that I can work my way through whatever difficulties I face.

When we have learned to manage our minds well, we can recognise and counter the negative narrative (on the left) by deliberately challenging the content and conclusions of this inner dialogue. Behind every negative perception is a preferred positive outcome. It's important to use the practice of 'flipping' to transform the focus of our self-talk to messages like those in the right column of the table above.

There are many stories about people who have transformed their circumstances through an unrelenting focus on what they want to accomplish, not on what they fear. However dire the predictive stories they heard or the 'stopper' messages they were invited to accept, they have created triumphant frames for themselves.

The particular story I would like to share with you is a personal one. It describes the experience of my friend Richard:

Richard was a captivating teacher and a powerful writer and speaker. He constantly encouraged others to improve their quality of life through positive frames and self-talk; through setting goals and believing in their power to achieve them. He was a storyteller whose stories opened avenues of possibility and hope to those who heard them.

In the prime of his life, Richard suffered a massive cerebral haemorrhage. For a while his doctors were not sure he would live. When he eventually regained consciousness, his brain had suffered serious damage. He was told he would never be able to work again, and to accept that he was functionally impaired - too much of his brain had been destroyed.

However, Richard gradually began to apply the principles he had personally lived and taught. Although his short-term memory was harmed, his reservoir of past learning and experience was still accessible. He used what he had: he employed disciplined self-talk; used positive imagery; channelled emotion into refusing to accept defeat; set goals and believed that he would attain them. When self-doubt and chronic exhaustion assailed him, he resolutely focused only on what he **could** do.

Within a few years he was again teaching and speaking in public. Although still hampered by the effects of his acquired brain injury, he returned to full-time work. It was a massive effort, but he summoned what he could and once again began to influence lives and inspire others.

Richard could have believed (and lived) the stories his doctors told him. He might have attended to the stopper messages all around him and given up. He chose instead to live the stories that shaped his own understanding of possibility and meaning. Whenever I think of Richard, I am reminded of the power of the stories we tell ourselves and the way we talk to ourselves.

Retired again now, Richard has returned to his writing, crafting insight and stories with his customary flair and humour. True to form, he is telling stories that offer hope, peace and inspiration to others who have acquired brain injuries. He is, and always will be, not only my friend but my inspirational mentor – a man for whom the word 'impossible' depicts not a truth but a challenge.

Self-talk can either damage or enable. The more we develop *LeaderMind* the more we become aware that this is a choice that we can make. If Richard, despite the physical damage to his brain, was able to steer his self-talk into his own healing and self-efficacy, so can we all.

As leaders we can also encourage the positive self-talk and associated learning efforts of our staff by taking the fear out of their attempts to extend their capability. Team members who know that they have nothing to fear from the awkward and unconfident early efforts that are inevitable when learning something new are many times more likely to feel encouraged rather than be assailed with self-doubt.

10.7
MENTAL IMAGING

Most of us are very good at imaging – making thought pictures. These are very powerful. A huge body of research shows that we can learn to refine or even learn a skill by visualising ourselves performing it. Any number of studies has found that a skilled performance can be 'practised' almost as well through visualisation drills as through actual physical practice. Athletes and artistic performers, public speakers and teachers, all use visualisation to 'practise' in their heads.

The reason this can be so effective is that our brain does not differentiate appreciably between visualising a successful performance and the actual performance. The same neural pathways are engaged in both. This has the potential for being a powerful mind-management tool – but a potentially harmful one if it is not well-managed. Rehearsing for success by seeing ourselves perform well is self-enhancing. Seeing ourselves failing is training for defeat.

When we know that our brain has this capacity to explore potential futures in advance, then good mind-management means giving it the right script. Initiating an inner screenplay in which we perform effectively and then rigorously sticking to that script is empowering.

10.8
SELF-CONCEPT

As you might guess, the way we come to see ourselves is made up of our interpretations of all of the experiences of life and is strongly influenced by the other 3 mental activities in this section: emotions, self-talk and imagery.

Robert Dilts[6] describes the powerful impact that 'how we see ourselves' (our self-perceived identity) has on our capability, our behaviour and how we respond to our environment. Our sense of identity - literally how we name or characterise ourselves - affects what we do and think and how we learn.

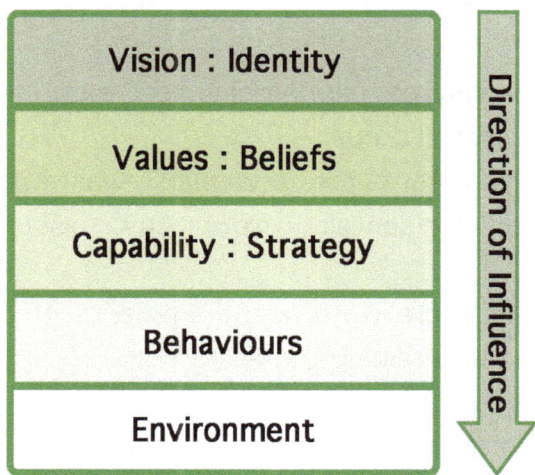

The level of identity is our sense of who we are. It is this perception that influences and organises our beliefs and values. As Dilts writes: "Our sense of identity also relates to our perception of ourselves in relation to the larger systems of which we are a part, determining our sense of 'role', 'purpose' and 'mission.'[7]

Although managing self-concept can seem difficult to master, it is largely based on creating a self-fulfilling conception of who we want to be. Creating this clear sense of our ideal self - the persona that we wish to inhabit as we live and work - is one of the most worthwhile design activities that we can ask our mind to perform.

My own struggle with self-identity was initially inhibited by my growing up experience of being the weedy little kid in glasses who was easy to push around! I saw myself as 'one-down' in my relationship with the people I perceived to be more confident; especially people who were large in size, voice or temperament.

For me, as for many people, learning to create and live a new persona had 4 critical steps:
i. Acknowledging that the persona I was inhabiting was constructed accidentally from past assumption and perceptions;
ii. Noticing that there were useful elements of present self-perception and retaining those;
iii. Imaging how it could be to live with a different sense of self and creating that new identity in imagination;
iv. Stepping into the new self with courage and learning to adopt beliefs, values, capabilities and behaviours that were congruent with the person that I was creating.

In my case, the process went something like this:

I. I realised that my 'inferior' identity was based on out-of-date self-perceptions. There was a time when being self-deprecating and seeing other people as 'superior' served me well. It was 'safer' to merge with the background. That time passed. If I was to thrive as a teacher and leader, and eventually in business, I needed a new perception of my identity.
II. I focused on the elements of my life where I experienced success and those where I wanted to excel in the future. I was a successful competitive runner, a passionately enthusiastic person and an intuitive thinker who frequently showed initiative. I wanted to build my sense of self around those things, as well as my wish to be effective in an executive role.
III. I imagined the person I would be proud to be, in as much detail and clarity as possible. I didn't throw out all of the old conceptions. I was selective. Humility had served me well and protected me from arrogance: It still needs to - and does. Regarding life and work as a 'competition' never did serve me well. I eschewed it. As a leader, I realised that being a person who takes delight in the achievements of others would better serve my purpose than self-promotion.
IV. I persisted in living myself into the new self, even when the 'old' me welled up. This was very much a case of 'fake it until you make it'. It has always been a work in progress, but one with which I have become increasingly comfortable. The more I have lived the new identity, the more I feel comfortable inside this sense of who I am.

As Dilts' levels model predicts, the new sense of who I am has led to the generation of renewed values and a more useful set of beliefs. Seeing myself differently, I acquired new capabilities and a raft of more effective behaviours. I feel comfortable in contexts that would once have intimidated me.

I can't say for sure that my experience of re-creating myself is a blueprint for everyone, but the literature suggests that it is. In particular, the process designed by Barnes Boffey[8], which he calls '*Reinventing Yourself*', is a powerful therapeutic process that helps people to identify the thought, actions, feelings and physiology that limit them, and then invites them to create more useful and powerful replacements.

As we move on to explore three key capabilities that extend leadership effectiveness, bear in mind that the personal learning and change that may be needed will often require us to access the mind-management tools that we have examined in this section: control of our emotions; talking to ourselves constructively; imaging our own effectiveness and inventing and exploiting a helpful personal self-concept.

CHAPTER ELEVEN

THREE GENERIC CAPABILITIES FOR LEADERS

"If human beings are perceived as potentials rather than problems, as possessing strengths instead of weaknesses, as unlimited rather that dull and unresponsive, then they thrive and grow to their capabilities."

Robert Conklin[1]

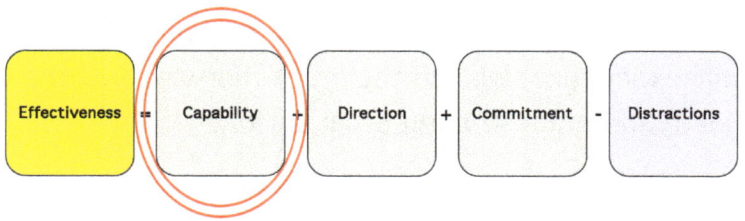

There are many context-dependent skills and abilities that leaders need for effectiveness in their particular profession or industry. These belong in the arena of specialist competencies and are not within the scope of this book.

In chapters Eleven to Fourteen I will present three generic leadership capabilities: a suite of generic leadership skills that will serve any leader in their own work context.

Perceptual Agility – The Ability to Direct Attention

"Wisdom comes from multiple perspectives."

Gregory Bateson[2]

In the context of leadership, developing the ability to see outside your own habitual mental map is massively helpful. Despite the limitations of our own perceptual system and personal experience, we can tap into other views of the world if we learn and practise perceptual agility.

11.1
Perceptual Agility

The practice that I describe as perceptual agility is the ability to attend to, and move between, whichever of the perceptual positions is most useful in any situation. Each of the perceptual positions is a way of paying attention to the world of experience. Each position provides an important perspective for leadership.

Perceptual Agility
The ability to move between Perceptual Positions at will to achieve optimum choice and flexibility

4th Perceptual Position: Zoomed out and able to adopt the perspective of the whole system.

3rd Perceptual Position: The ability to disassociate and take the helicopter view.

2nd Perceptual Position: The ability to model the thinking of another person. Empathetic rapport.

1st Perceptual Position: The self-referencing position. Totally associated. Absorbed in own thinking.

1st Perceptual Position is self-focused. In this position we pay attention to our own thoughts, ideas and values and on our own current priorities. Having a clear understanding of our own 1st position is critical for self-awareness and self-management. It enables us to be clear about what we know and believe. It underpins the honest assertiveness that is essential to personal integrity. But however well we know ourselves, the boundaries of 1st Perceptual Position are always defined by the limitations of our own experience and the current focus of our thinking.

We all express opinions and make judgments from this primary way of attending to the world – but this position limits us. In '1st position' we know only what we know, and we consider every situation from the perspective of self. Our own emotions can be intrusive when we are self-focused and are not always useful features of our leadership perspective. As leaders, we need a greater variety of ways in which to pay attention!

In 2nd Perceptual Position, we deliberately focus on the perceived world of other people. We do our best to think our way into the brains of others. The primary tool of 2nd Perceptual Position is listening – listening without judgment and with genuine curiosity: but it's more than listening. In 2nd position we also use our other senses to decode the messages we perceive from the total behaviour of the other person. We notice their physiology and actions, as well as listening to their words and tone of voice. As our expertise in 2nd position grows, we get a sense of what is important to the other person and why; of what things excite and discourage them' of what incidents and encounters mean through the lenses of their experience.

Using 2nd position takes effort and practice for most of us. In natural mode (1st position) we are habitually self-referencing creatures, processing whatever is said and done by other people through our own perceptual system. Whatever we hear or see, our own thoughts and interpretations flood unbidden into our consciousness, cutting off the flow of information that we receive from other people. To develop 2nd position we have to keep refocusing our attention on what we are hearing or seeing from the other person. When our own thoughts pop into our heads (as they certainly will) we have to learn to allow them to pass through our consciousness like bubbles rising to the surface of a lake, without examining them or paying any attention to them. A useful way of attending in 2nd position is to think of yourself as looking over someone else's shoulder at the world - as if from inside their mind.

Developing 2nd position radically expands our understanding of the 'universes' that are the experience of our staff or colleagues. Once we are conscious of 2nd position and begin to practise it, our empathic connection with other people and their different way of perceiving 'reality' expands our own awareness. With the agility to move between 1st and 2nd positions at will, we begin to acquire both a new way of seeing things and an important tool of mind-management. We can move beyond our own 'rightness' and certainty in order to incorporate the perspectives of our colleagues and associates.

11.2
ZOOMING OUT

Adding **3rd Perceptual Position** to our repertoire is powerful in another way. In 3rd position we attend to what is happening as if we are a detached observer simply describing what is going on. In 3rd position we can use the metaphor of a fly on the ceiling or a 'helicopter view' to explain what is happening. Try this simple exercise: wherever you are as you read this, imagine you are out of your own body describing what can be seen. Remember that as an observer, you will not be accessing your own thinking - simply describing what someone standing a few metres away might see.

Or, in another way of practising and appreciating 3rd position - think back to a stressful interpersonal encounter from your recent past and simply describe what happened. Don't try to explain what each person in the scenario might have been thinking or feeling - simply describe what an impartial observer might report.

What we notice in 3rd Perceptual Position, is that emotion disappears (or at the least is diminished). Think how useful this can be to the leader. Faced with one of the many highly emotive and challenging situations in which our own feelings can trigger defensiveness or distress, adopting 3rd position is liberating!

As an observer, we can watch ourselves and the situation dispassionately and make reasoned choices about how this person we are watching (ourselves) can behave to be most effective.

3rd position takes practice. To be an observer of a situation that includes yourself requires a quite deliberate shift from emotional behaviour into a detached thinking mode. I like to assist myself in this shift by quite deliberately saying to myself, (adopting a professorial tone in my internal dialogue): "If someone was watching this what they would see is ......" and describing everything that an observer would notice.

Another way of getting firmly into 3rd Position is to use a metaphor or analogy to describe what is happening. A colleague, an idealist who has faced many challenges in his leadership and has been the subject of a great deal of public criticism, shared with me his 3rd position metaphor of waves breaking against a rocky headland. The pounding waves shape his character and refine his thinking but, like the rocky promontory, he is unyielding about the core values and moral purpose that are the essence of his leadership influence.

As 3rd position becomes well developed, our perceptual agility becomes even more useful. In any complex situation, it is potent to be able to get in touch with your own purpose and beliefs, but also to deeply appreciate the different perspectives of others and (when required) adopt the detached perspective of 3rd position.

Finally, there is what I regard as the quintessential leadership viewpoint – **4th Perceptual Position**. In 4th position, we look at the situation, the challenge or the problem from the point of view of the organisation or team we lead. We zoom out from our own concerns and those of our colleagues to ask ourselves: "What would be best for the business?" or "What will help this school to thrive?"

When we adopt 4th Perceptual Position it is vital to put aside ambition and ego in order to include an objective 3rd position of the situation. This is the time to take a long-term perspective and to ask ourselves "What's really in the best interests of the whole institution?"

The benefits of this act of will, this stepping away from the personal affiliations of all the people in the business (including oneself) are surprising. I am often taken aback at the difference it makes to a challenging issue when I zoom out and use 4th Perceptual Position. This position takes us out of the personal tunnel vision that inhibits us all as leaders. The sense of 'rightness' with which we tend to varnish our own beliefs fades away and we see important issues with clarity.

Of course, in 4th perceptual position we can choose how far to zoom out. I have met a school Principal who often takes the perspective of 'what is the way forward that could benefit every child in every school if it becomes universally applied'. I read about a corporate leader who claims to make his decisions based on 'what's best for the future of the world?'.

Combining 4th position with the other 3 positions provides even greater perceptual agility, adding to the other three the capacity to take a 'big picture' perspective.

Together, the perceptual positions and the ability to move between them with agility will assist you with the first three orders of leadership effectiveness: They help you to manage yourself; enable you to see how and when to influence others; and they provide an important structure for focusing the deliberations of your team.

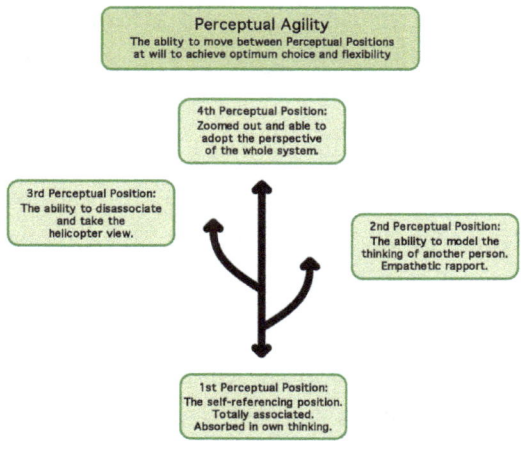

CHAPTER TWELVE

BUILDING CAPACITY IN OTHERS THROUGH COACHING

"Effective Leaders leave a trail of capability in their wake."

R.G. Pierre[1]

12.1
COACHING

Coaching is a skill that draws heavily on 2nd Perceptual Position. We can use it to help anyone in our team or business to grow in capacity and add value to our pool of capability.

Coaching requires 2nd Perceptual Position because the focus of coaching is the coachee (i.e. the person we are coaching), not ourselves. In the first section of the book we saw how important it is for leaders to understand and accept the paradox of power. As leaders, we can achieve nothing by ourselves. Productivity and effectiveness, client service, enterprise, initiative - all those things that help a business to thrive - come from the work of our staff. Leadership success is not distinct from building capacity: one is dependent on the other. As R.G. Pierre reminds us: "Effective leaders leave a trail of capability in their wake.".

There are three principal tools for building capacity: Teaching, mentoring and coaching. Of these three, the most useful for a leader is coaching. As you read that, some of you might think it's a big call, so I would like to clarify what I mean.

Teaching and mentoring require a significant level of 'technical' expertise. Coaches on the other hand are expert question askers! The coach does not need to know the intricacies of a colleague's work in order to coach effectively. What the coach *does* need is the ability to evoke trust and to use enquiry in a way that stimulates the thinking of the coachee.

'Teaching' our staff becomes increasingly problematic with each leadership promotion or increase in our responsibilities. Although we may have earned our first leadership role at least in part through high levels of technical expertise, once we have a leadership focus, we don't last long at the cutting edge of technical proficiency. That level of personal skill is no longer central to our role, so we rarely have the credibility to teach a staff member how to do a better job - unless their own technical skills are at quite a low level.

Similarly, although we may be able to mentor our colleagues to extend their leadership capability, we are rarely plausible mentors in the specific expertise required of the work they do.

However, we can coach anyone irrespective of their speciality. All of the specifics of what to do and how to do it are in the head of the coachee. As coach, our role is to unlock the arteries of possibility that run through the mind of the individual or group that we are coaching. I have coached individuals whose expertise was in technology, sales, environmental protection and employee placement. I have no significant knowledge of any of these fields. I was still able to be an effective coach.

12.2
COACHING THE WAY THE MIND WORKS

Knowing the way in which the human mind works provides us with the cues we need to be effective coaches. As we saw in Section Two, the source of motivation is closing the gap between what we 'want' (i.e. one or more features of our ideal world) and what we perceive to be happening. When we are coaching someone, our job is to help **them** close the gap between what **they** want and what **they** perceive is happening.

It follows that the first step in coaching is to help the coachee identify with clarity what it is that they want (i.e. what their goal is, what they think will improve their situation).

The coaching process[1] builds on the identification of a clear 'want' by enquiring:
- What are you doing to get what you want?
- Is it working or do you need to do something else?
- What other options are there?
- Create a plan for new behaviours.

The procedures-in-action can be illustrated by this dialogue between an assistant manager and one of his team leaders:

AM "You seem a bit frustrated with lack of progress recently?"

TL "As a team, we have agreed that we need to develop different ways of addressing some of the problems that are holding us up, but nobody is making any suggestions. I am the only one who appears willing to come up with new ideas."

AM *(paraphrases)*: "You would like to see other team members take the initiative?"

TL "Yes, it's unreasonable for the team to expect me to come up with all the new options."

AM "How would things be different if new initiatives were being suggested by several of your team members?"

TL *(pauses)* "Well, we would be making progress. And people would not be leaving it all to me."

AM "And that's important to you – that other team members participate fully in identifying and exploring even more effective ways of tackling the issues?"

TL "Yes. If everyone took ownership, we would have a much more creative vibe happening. Lots of new possibilities might start popping up."

AM "And how would you be seeing your role if that level of creative originality was coming from the team?"

TL "It would be a weight off my mind! I would feel as if responsibility was being willingly shared instead of always being on my shoulders."

At this point, the Assistant Manager believes his colleague has enough clarity about what she wants to achieve. The next phase of the procedure is to find out what the Team Leader has been doing to achieve what she wants and ask her to self-evaluate her current behaviours.

AM "Well, what have you been doing to encourage the team to show high levels of creative initiative and share the responsibility for success?"

TL "I have mentioned it a couple of times in team meetings…"

AM "Has that been enough?"

TL "Well, obviously not. But it's hard to know what else I can do without admitting I am struggling. After all, it is really my responsibility."

AM "So, because you think you should be responsible you are reluctant to say you need more help from them?
Is approaching the situation in that way moving things in the direction you want?"

TL "No… So, you think I should just be upfront and tell them I need help?"

AM "How could it hurt? You're not happy with how things are."

TL "But I would still need to make it clear that everything has to come through me. If team members just try things without some analysis and coordination, it could get pretty chaotic."

AM "Hmm. It seems like you want to be in control as well. Which is more important to you: being in control, or team members taking initiative?"

TL "When you put it like that… *(long pause)* But what if there are some stuff ups?"

AM "Can you have creativity and progress without experimenting and taking some risks?"

TL "Perhaps not. Ok, almost certainly not. So, you think I should just encourage people to try new approaches and be prepare to accept that there will be some mistakes and dead ends?"

AM "Will it be better than what's happening now? After all, you do want team members to take initiative. Is that possible without giving up some control?"

TL "No. I see that now. Maybe I have been stifling initiative by insisting that everything comes through me."

AM *(allows the silence to give the TL time to think)*

TL "It seems as if I have to be prepared to tell my team to go for it: try out any ideas that they have; maybe encourage a bit of crazy experimentation"

AM "Can you do that?"

TL "I can!"

The exploration of what the Team Leader has been doing and the persistent self-evaluation questions have led to a new possibility. The Assistant Manager can now help his colleague by checking to see if there are other options, and then by helping her to turn her intentions into specific actions.

AM "Is there anything else you can could do to encourage initiative and responsibility in the team?"

TL "Well, thinking about it, there was a suggestion by Simon that I shut down because I did not think it would work. Maybe I can show everyone I am taking a new approach by going back to him and encouraging him to try out his ideas."

AM "Are you prepared to do that?"

TL "Yes, I am. I think that would show that I am trying a new way of encouraging team initiative."

AM "Anything else?"

TL "I think someone may ask – what will happen if we try something and it doesn't work? They will be worried about that I think."

AM "How will you deal with that concern?"

TL "I think I should say that I know we will all make mistakes. And when we do, we should discuss what happened and work out what there is to learn from them?"

AM "How do you feel about that?"

TL "I think that would work. It will help the whole team get involved in problem-solving in a more active way. I like that idea."

AM "So, to summarise. You have suggested being explicit with the team about needing help; going back to Simon's suggestion and encouraging him to run with it; and implementing a protocol for dealing with initiatives that are not successful.
Which of those things will you do?"

TL "All of them. I think that's a package of things that will make it clear to the team that I want us to go in a new direction. And I think I will also ask the team if there is anything else they would like me to do to support them in this new way of approaching problems."

This looks like a good suite of options. The Assistant Manager did not leave it there: at present the intentions are good but they are not yet actions. To conclude the coaching conversation, the Manager asked a few more questions to check if the plan that the Team Leader has come up with is:

Specific: Specifically, what will she say and do?

Time-framed: When will she do or say these things?
Measurable: How will she know whether these options are working?

This leaves out two of the components of the most common acronym for an effective plan (S.M.A.R.T. – Specific, Measurable, Attractive, Realistic and Time-Framed). In practice, as often happens during a coaching conversation, the questions have already elicited that the proposal is attractive and realistic, so the Manager did not ask about these aspects.

12.3
FEATURES OF A SUCCESSFUL COACHING CONVERSATION

As we look back on this example of a coaching conversation, there are some aspects of it that we should notice and look at more closely.

- The 'Want' must be positive.
- The 'Want' must be explored thoroughly enough to increase clarity and motivation.
- Paraphrasing is an important feature of the exploration of the Want – and it helps to keep the coach in 2nd Perceptual Position.
- Self-evaluation is crucial to an effective coaching conversation.

Let's look at each of these in turn:

12.4
THE WANT MUST BE POSITIVE:

If we look back to Section Two, we notice that there are two kinds of motivation. There is what we can call 'moving towards' motivation: closing the gap between what we want and what we perceive. There is also 'moving away from' motivation: when we are trying to avoid something we don't want.

A coaching conversation only works when we identify a want or a goal to move towards. This means that a 'don't want' (a negative perception) has to be re-framed as a positive. This is always possible because every 'don't want' in our perception is matched by a preferred situation ('a want'), even though this is not always obvious to the coachee.

As we coach someone, it is important to listen for the 'don't want' - the negative perception - and help the coachee work out the positive preference that goes with it. You will notice that, in the conversation between the Assistant Manager and the Team Leader, the Team Leader led with her negative perceptions of the team:
"No-one is making any suggestions" and "It's unreasonable to expect me to come up with all of the new options".
The Manager re-frames these as positive wants:
"You would like to see other team members take the initiative?" and
"How would things be different if new initiatives were being suggested by team members?"

As previously mentioned, This is what my colleague, Judy Hatswell, describes as 'Flipping': hearing what is NOT wanted and recognising the positive preference that is the flip side of that negative.

The ability to reframe to the positive, even when the coachee tells you what they don't want, is an essential coaching skill.

Many people have more clarity about the circumstances or behaviour they dislike than what they actually want in a situation. It's a natural feature of how the brain works. However, there is always an ideal world conception associated with a 'don't want' statement, even when the coachee is not consciously aware of it.

Knowing this, we can listen attentively for these negative perceptions during a coaching conversation and 'flip' them towards the ideal or preferred mental images.

I find it useful, (both as a self-management discipline and as a practising coach) to reflect on the 'don't wants' in my own life. I'm very aware that I dislike it when people don't follow through with their commitments; when people are argumentative or critical; or (on a more trivial level) when the weather is cold or rainy! These 'don't likes' are the flip side of my personal commitment to professionalism and always doing my best; my preference for harmony and understanding - and my love of sunshine!

Practising 'the flip' on ourselves helps us to master it. As an exercise, try listing all of the things that are 'wrong' with your present experience of life. Then, quite deliberately and reflectively, use these negative perceptions to work out your own conceptions of quality - the 'ideal' pictures that you carry in your head. This exercise helps us to realise how important our own quality pictures are to us, and how easy it is to feel dissatisfied when these conceptions of how things should be are not matched by our present experience. It's also a reflective practice that helps us create the future we prefer!

The reason that identifying the positive on the other side of the 'don't want' is so important for coaching procedure is that these expressions of what we 'don't want' are not useful in helping the coachee to get what they do want – to achieve a goal or improve their life or work situation. To achieve a change, the coachee must take responsibility for making a change. What the coach does is to help the coachee navigate towards accepting responsibility for making a change that will make a difference.

As pointed out by Karpman[2], all dysfunctional behaviour is generated by one or another irresponsible way of dealing with the (inevitable) problems of life.

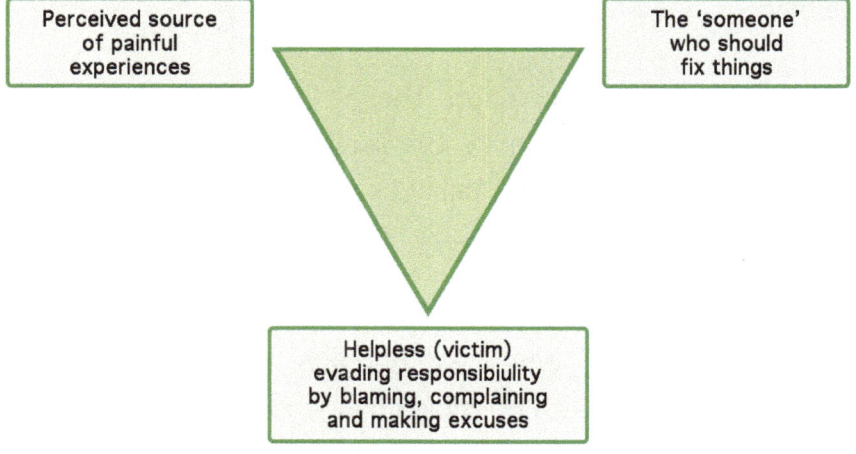

We can blame someone else (or the vicissitudes of life); make excuses for ourselves; or complain about the unfairness or unreasonableness of it all. None of these is empowering.

'The Flip' is a crucial step towards responsibility because it helps the coachee to focus on what they do want instead of what they feel is wrong.

12.5
GAINING CLARITY ABOUT THE WANT

Even when the goal or want is expressed as a positive, gaining greater clarity is always useful. With clarity, the coachee will gain greater understanding of:
- What they really want;
- What difference the improvement will make;
- Why achieving this change is so important to them;
- The impact that a change will have on their own wellbeing.

Working deliberately through these levels of clarity and significance tends to enhance the likelihood that the coachee will accept responsibility for making a change and intensify their motivation to do so.

There is a structure to these questions that is derived from the levels of perception. When we perceive something only as useful information or as a possible change in our circumstances, there is a relatively low level of motivation attached to it. When the change is valued or meaningful, the associated motivation is greater. When it has ramifications for our own sense of wellbeing, our self-certainty or self-efficacy, the motivation level is highest.

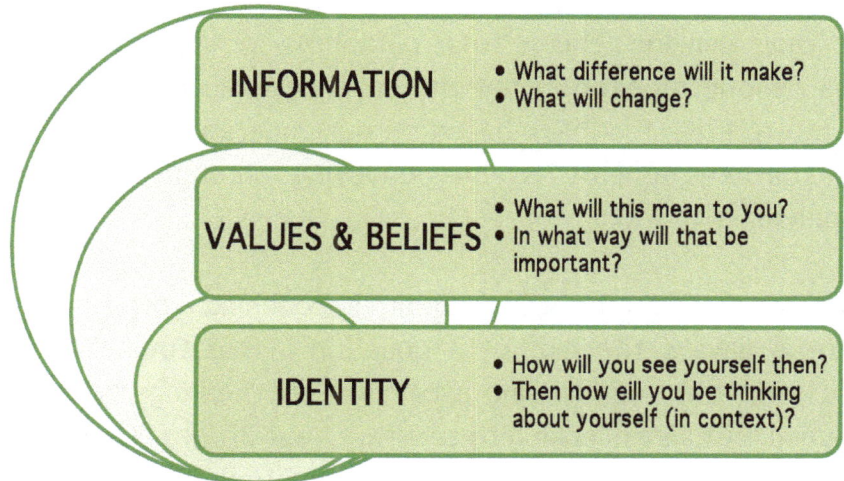

The questions to increase clarity, which were embedded in the conversation between the Team Leader and Assistant Manager, follow this pattern.

Gaining clarity by asking questions at these deeper levels (information, values, identity) helps the coachee to get in touch with their deepest wants. Using these questions, we can descend a spiral staircase into the most profound levels of the person's Quality World.

12.6
THE IMPORTANCE OF PARAPHRASING

Paraphrasing the coachee's last reply helps the coaching process in two ways:
- It helps the coachee to 'hear' and refine his or her own responses to the questions.

- It helps the coach to stay in 2nd Perceptual Position. Remember that in 2nd Perceptual Position we are always trying to understand what the other person means; to delve deeply into their thinking. This is what paraphrasing helps us with. It goes beyond repeating what the coachee has said; it is more like interpretive feedback based on our understanding of what the coachee appears to be conveying through their last response.

When we are paraphrasing during a coaching conversation, there is always the hint of a question in our tone. We are reflecting and summarising what we are hearing from the coachee, but also checking to see if we have it right. That slight suggestion of a question in our voice encourages the coachee to correct us, or to further clarify their own thinking.

The rhythm of the coaching conversation follows the pattern that you will have noticed in the example at the start of this chapter. Each question contains a paraphrase of the last thing that the coachee says. To help the conversation sound natural, it's best to avoid introducing the paraphrase with 'I hear you saying that' or 'What you are saying is'. Instead, simply incorporate the paraphrase into the sentence either at the start as in: "If team members took more responsibility, how would things be better for you?" or after the question, such as "What would it mean to you if team members took more responsibility?"

12.7
SELF-EVALUATION:
THE FULCRUM OF THE COACHING CONVERSATION

The part of the coaching conversation that creates the most leverage for acceptance of responsibility and change is the part containing the self-evaluation questions. It's the way to help the coachee jolt their thinking out of the habits of mind that are limiting their capability.

It may seem self-evident that doing the same thing as we have been doing without success is unlikely to lead to a different future outcome. (The aphorism that 'doing the same thing over and over again, but expecting a different result, is akin to insanity' is often attributed to Einstein). However, once we get used to thinking about or doing something in a particular way it easily becomes habitual and our mind can be limited by that pattern of thought. It's for this reason that a successful coaching conversation always pivots on well-presented self-evaluation questions. When the coachee identifies their own behaviours and admits to themselves that these are not leading to the desired want or outcome, their thinking shifts.

Questions that gently probe for a self-evaluation such as: "Is that helping you?"; "Has that been taking you closer to what you want – or further away?"; Is that working?"; "Is that making things better or worse?" – these questions chip away at the foundations of well-established behaviours.

It sometimes takes time and patience by the coach for self-evaluation questions to penetrate to the level of consciousness needed for a change. For example, I recall coaching a colleague in a senior position whose confidence was continually eroded by her own negative self-talk - which was giving undue credence to the opinions of a few of her staff. Over several coaching conversations, I asked in many different ways whether her self-talk was helping her? Somehow, she always seems to dismiss or ignore the question.

Then one day, just as we began the conversation, she told me again about her fear that these colleagues did not respect her previous experience (a repeated theme of her self-talk). After a pause I asked (as I had many times before): "How useful is it when you think like that?"

This time, she heard me! Her whole demeanour changed. She sat up and stared at me with a startled expression. "It's not bloody useful at all she said!" And from that moment on, being a talented leader and basically a strong-minded person, she began to focus on the actual value of her past experience rather than the critical opinions of a small number of people. Some self-evaluation questions may be like a slow-burning fuse. Eventually they will ignite new thinking.

The important thing to remember is that this process of examining behaviour, and self-evaluating, truly is the fulcrum for change. Without it, many empathic conversations lead the coachee to a sense of being understood – but there is no change. The self-evaluation questions are the engine-room of coaching.

Sometimes I am asked if the coach can offer an evaluation if the coachee seems reluctant to examine themselves. The answer (unless there is a very high level of trust and respect in the relationship) is a qualified negative! Telling someone that: "Your behaviour is not working to produce the desired result" usually triggers defence. As we saw in Section Two, the social survival instinct is ever alert to a put-down or threat to our autonomy or competence. We change and expand our repertoire of behaviours when our **internal** processing provides the urge to do so: when we see for ourselves that the quality we seek is only attainable when our behaviour changes. Thoughts that are generated outside our own mind rarely carry the conviction of our own insight, unless the level of mutual respect between coach and coachee is very high.

12.8
ANOTHER EXAMPLE

Perhaps the best way to close this chapter is to provide another example of a coaching conversation that illustrates all of the features described above.

This time the conversation is between a school Principal (P) and the Head Teacher of Science in her school.

> HT "Thanks for seeing me. I would appreciate your advice. I think I should have a straight talk with Wendy, but she is so hard to communicate with!"
>
> P "There are issues that you want to address with Wendy, and you want to get it right?"
>
> HT "Yes. She has been so critical and grumpy with everyone recently. Something changed while I was away

	on leave. She was fine before then, but now she is really eroding the unity of the department."
P	"You are worried about the effect she is having on the way people work together? – and what you would like is to have the whole team collaborating and supporting each other?"
HT	"Yes - and that includes Wendy. She does have great ideas when she wants to share."
P	"Right. So, if that were happening – if the whole team were cooperating and helping each other, including Wendy - what would change for you all?"
HT	"That's easy! There would be less grumbling, people would say what they think without fear of criticism; team meetings would be more relaxed; it would all be more light-hearted … we'd enjoy working together!"
P	"It would mean a lot to you to re-create that sense of cohesion and participation? And have more fun?"
HT	"It would mean a lot. We really depend on everyone participating and sharing if we are going to get the best outcomes for the students. We all have different strengths and expertise - but at present, we are tending to work alone rather than help each other."
P	"So, it's very important to you to create an open environment in which team members can consult each other; draw on each other's strengths and be confident that their contribution will be appreciated?"
HT	"It's absolutely vital!"
P	"How will you see yourself when you have re-created that sense of team?"
HT	"If I can … *(pause)* I hear what you are saying. <u>When</u> we are working well as a team, I will feel more relaxed and look forward to the friendliness and respect of the

	team. I will look forward to coming to work much more than I do at the moment."
P	"You have been concerned about this for a few weeks. What have you been doing to re-create the sense of team that you will love working with?"
HT	"Well, as you say – worrying a lot!"
P	"Is that helping?"
HT	*(with a wry smile)* "Not at all!"
P	"Have you given anything else a try?"
HT	"At our meeting on Tuesday, I did talk to the whole team about the importance of sharing and being supportive of each other. But that actually seemed to shut everyone down. Nobody said anything. Wendy stared at the table, and everyone else looked at her and then looked away."
P	"So … thinking about that. Did you learn anything that might help you?"
HT	"Only that other people might be thinking that Wendy is the 'problem' as well; and that they are reluctant to say anything in case it makes things worse."
P	"It sounds as if there is a lot going on, but it's based on the interpretation of silences! Is that moving you on or just complicating things further?"
HT	"It's not making any difference. Perhaps it's making things less clear."
P	"Let me summarise. You know that you are a long way from the open supportive culture that you want in your department. It's affecting how you and your team members feel about their work, and also the effectiveness of the team. You are not really sure what's going on though - Is that right?"

HT	"You're right – and I am afraid that if I know what's really going on, I won't know how to deal with it."
P	"Are you dealing with it now?"
HT	*(Shakes his head)* "No."
P	"Is guessing (but not asking) making any positive difference?"
HT	"You think I should talk to Wendy?"
P	"What do you think?"
HT	"I think I do have to talk with Wendy."
P	"But, if we go back to the start of this conversation, I think I remember that you were reluctant to do this because you don't want to make things worse?"
HT	"That's exactly right."
P	"So, are you clear about what Wendy thinks about the importance of sharing, collaborating, being supportive of team members, having fun together?"
HT	"No."
P	"Would it hurt to find out?"
HT	"If she will tell me, it will help."
P	"Do you have some thoughts about how to approach the conversation so that she will be open with you?"
HT	"If she thinks I am criticising her she gets angry."
P	"Do you need to be critical? Can you think of another way to approach it?"
HT	"I could ask her to help me: tell her that I am worried about the team and ask her what she would suggest that we do in order to get a better team environment?"
P	"Could you do that?"
HT	"Yes. I don't think she will be defensive about that, especially if I make the conversation quite informal."
P	"How will you do that?"

HT	"I'll ask her if she wants to go for a coffee because I need to ask her advice."
P	*(nods, but says nothing)*
HT	"Then, if she will talk, I will listen to what she says and try to understand what she is thinking. I won't argue with her. As you always say – her perception is her perception."
P	"Whatever comes from this discussion, do you think you will be better able to deal with the situation?"
HT	"I think so. If I know what is really going on for Wendy I hope that I will be able to work out what to do next."
P	"So, will you do this?"
HT	"Yes. I will invite her for a coffee tomorrow. I know we both have a preparation period before lunch."
P	"Let me know how it goes."

I chose this example - not only because it illustrates the skills embedded in a coaching conversation - but also because it illustrates a number of key realities about coaching in general:

1. There is not always a 'solution' as a result of a single coaching interaction. The aim of coaching is to help the person to move their thinking along to a point where the situation is clarified and further progress towards the 'really want' becomes increasingly possible.

2. Coaching is rarely a 'one-off' activity. One can imagine that the Head Teacher might return (with greater understanding of the situation) to talk through 'next steps' with his coach. At times, what is presented here as a single conversation may - in the context of two busy people – have actually occupied several shorter conversations.

3. As you read through the conversation, you will notice that the Principal as Coach does not give advice – even though the Head Teacher asks for it. She flips the first few negative perceptions, and then asks clarifying questions to help the Head Teacher understand what he wants. After that, almost everything that we hear from her invites the Head Teacher to self-evaluate. It's not that there is a 'rule' that the coach never makes a suggestion. It's just that it's far more effective if all the thinking is done through the mental processing of the person who will be taking action. Only if the coachee has no idea what to do (and if the coach has expertise and is trusted and respected) will a suggestion sometimes be useful.

CHAPTER THIRTEEN

CREATING TEAM

If you want to go fast, go alone. If you want to go far, go together!

Kenyan proverb

13.1
TEAM

The third generic capability I have chosen to highlight is the ability to create team.

It's commonplace for leaders to describe the group of people they supervise as 'my team'. I do it myself. Team is one of those group nouns that carries a tick of approval with it. 'My team' has a ring to it that 'my staff' or 'the workforce' lacks. However, the generic use of 'team' distracts us from the purpose and payoff of creating team: a distinctive and productive way of working together.

There is a difference between a team and a group of people working successfully in the same enterprise. I like to describe it this way: if people have the expertise to independently deliver all that is needed from them by the organisation, they don't need to be a team. Indeed, expending energy to build a team when one is not required erodes their effectiveness.

If however, their best work can only be delivered when group members depend on each other, and if they can either enhance or inhibit each other's effectiveness by the quality of their individual work, then a team is needed.

It follows that, before spending any time on creating team, we should always be sure that it will be worth the effort: that there will be a pay-off in the productivity and effectiveness of the work as a result - because truly creating team (or teams) takes time and effort. Creating team is a capability that is eminently learnable but deceptively difficult. When team is needed, creating and sustaining it becomes one of the leader's inescapable priorities.

13.2
A TEAM REQUIRES 'TEAMING'

You may have noticed that I write about creating team, not creating *a team*. This is a purposeful idiosyncrasy. I am using this form of words for emphasis.

If we talk about 'creating a team' it implies a certain passivity among those who will become team members – as if the entity we call the 'team' team is somehow independent of the intention, values and commitment of its members. It supports the presupposition that there can be an entity 'the team' to which team members are added or recruited.

Conversely, creating team brings with it the imperative that teaming (a very participatory activity) is central to the project of creating team. There can be no team without teaming: without the willing participation of team members to enter this distinctive relationship.

13.3
What Team is:

What then are the capabilities that a leader can develop in order to enhance their capability to create team?

From the reading, research and experience that comes from a lifetime of working with teams (both successfully and unsuccessfully) these six (perhaps surprising) necessities stand out:
- Ability to formulate a shared purpose;
- Appreciation and encouragement of team member individuality and autonomy;
- The capacity to identify the Interdependence of team members;
- Thoughtful use of consensus decision-making;
- A commitment to encouraging open and comprehensive communication;
- The ability to encourage constructive dispute and deep thinking.

There are strong connections between each of these capabilities and each provides its own clue about the creation of team. They are not in an order of priority: they are all important. We will reflect on each of them independently before examining the complexity of putting them all together

13.4
FORMULATING SHARED PURPOSE

When I talk with groups of leaders -either in my workshops or in coaching conversations -shared purpose is always identified as a key feature of team creation.

This is not simply the purpose of the company or institution per se. It means that the team itself must have an identifiable purpose, a reason for its work together. The team's purpose will contribute to the goals of the whole organisation but will also describe the specific contribution of the team to the achievement of those goals or outcomes. For example, the I.T. team in a business might be committed to working together to develop technology solutions that will not only enhance business outcomes but also provide the most user-friendly solutions possible for other arms of the business to use.

From this example, we can see that the framing of the purpose is of great significance for its value to the team and to the whole organisation. An I.T. team whose purpose was simply to develop 'cutting edge' technology solutions might not emphasise their ease of use, or their application by workers in other parts of the business. Purpose always drives function. Getting the purpose right makes a difference to what people do; to how they work together, and to the criteria that they use in making decisions.

It's the ability to formulate this shared purpose that's especially important for team leadership. Often the first step in this is to manage our own strong opinions. Engaging team members in the process of proposing, examining and deciding on a statement of purpose that really drives the activity of the team involves skilful use of perceptual agility. As leaders, we have to remain in 2nd position to allow all options to be presented, and 3rd position to manage negotiation between apparently competing options. We also require the judgment to know when to judiciously insert our own (1st Position) viewpoints, as well as the ability to keep taking the discussion to 4th Perceptual Position so that it's about what's best for the business, rather than for any individual.

In this process, what emerges is not a purpose developed by the team leader for team members to 'buy into'. It's the collaborative formulation of a driving purpose that will engage every team member. The purpose of a team must be shared, or it will fail to harness the autonomous motivation of each team member.

13.5
THE 'I' IN TEAM:
APPRECIATING INDIVIDUALITY AND AUTONOMY

One of the most misleading and thoughtless clichés that pervades the mythology around teams is that 'there is no 'I' in team'!

While this cliché draws on a superficial truth about the spelling of the actual word, it misses the whole point of team. If team members were anonymous components of a collective - simply sublimating their individuality and expertise to an undifferentiated entity - then this hackneyed phrase would have validity. But this conception of a team is more like a human blancmange than a vigorous collaboration of individuals with their own expertise, opinion and contribution to make.

A real team draws on the disparate talents and personal strength of individuals, so that the contribution of each plays a part in the effectiveness of the whole team.

In developing and encouraging effective team behaviour, we draw on our understanding of the way in which humans are motivated. All our motivation comes from the inside; from our urge to satisfy our genetic needs.

Every individual is internally motivated to satisfy their need for power and their need for autonomy. The first entails the self-perception of each individual that they are important, competent, significant and successful. It means that the status of a team member has to be far more than an instrument of the collective. Individuals will work energetically in a team when they can see that the team offers opportunities for success and for achievements that add to whatever they can attain as individuals. As one colleague told me: "If the team doesn't need my talent it does not need me. I have more important things to do than fitting in to the team for the sake of 'fake unity'."

Similarly, our need for autonomy drives us towards self-determination, to make individual choices. We are energised participants in whatever we do willingly, rarely in what we feel compelled to do through duty or by compliance. By definition then 'going along to get along' is anathema to the need satisfaction of independent and effective team members.

What this means is that there are many 'I's in team – as many as there are team members. The team must be designed and managed as a collective which harnesses rather than sublimates the individual gifts of its members. When the team is formed - and re-formed as its members change - introducing team members to each other in a way that emphasises what is distinctive about each; working in ways that celebrate what each knows and can do (even appreciating the unorthodox) these are the approaches that bring together the individuals in a team to work towards a shared purpose.

13.6
IDENTIFYING AND NURTURING INTERDEPENDENCE.

It follows, from what has been said about team in the last few pages, that team works when its members are interdependent – when they can rely on each other for the contribution that each makes to the other. Every individual (including yourself as team leader) will engage most strongly with work of the team when they know how they benefit from it.

One of the first jobs of a team leader is to devote enough time to discussion and exploration so that these interdependencies can be identified. This is especially important when we take on leadership of a team where team members are used to working independently; getting on with their own jobs without communicating with each other or drawing on the knowledge and skill of team members. If individuals are used to working solo, the advantages of working with each other are not always obvious.

Blindness to the advantages of collaborative interdependence is often exacerbated by leaders who think that the way to get the best from team members is to encourage competition between them. The way competition works is through the creation of losers (or how can there be winners?). Those who perceive themselves as losers rarely bring their 'A game' to their work. Collaborative inter-dependence emphasises both mutual and individual benefit – 'best for me **and** best for us'.

In searching for and identifying the important inter-dependencies of the team, the leader's most useful capability is to be a master question-asker. Questions that encourage team members to identify and appreciate their interdependence include:
- What is it that any one of us can do which would enhance the productivity of another?
- How and when do some of us actually interfere with or impede the work of another? (Leaders must be prepared for honest answers to this question!)
- What are the overlapping aspects of our individual work?
- If each of us could learn the skills we respect in each other, how would we benefit?
- How can we help each other to think in 4th Perceptual Position when making decisions?
- What can we learn from each other?
- What do we need to know about each other's work?

- Are there resources that we share (human and material) that we can co-manage to advantage?
- What can our 'clients-in-common' benefit if we work together?
- What is the capacity we need to build around ourselves, and how can we collaborate to develop it?
- What do we need to know from each other?
- What kind of communication between us (in and out of team meetings) can be mutually beneficial?

The suggestion is not that team members are confronted by an avalanche of such questions. It will generally be more productive if, during the forming phases of team development, a selection of such questions is asked; and the answers gently explored as the opportunity for them arises.

Once the impetus for exploring team interdependence has been initiated by the leader, team members often accept the invitation to continue this search for mutual effectiveness.

13.7
Consensus Decision-Making

It's unrealistic to divorce the way that a team makes decisions from the way that the team operates. If we have encouraged strong individual contribution and personal engagement, then team members will want (and most likely expect) a voice in team decisions.

There are three levels of participatory decision-making, all of which borrow from a family of descriptors that are often used almost interchangeably, but which are actually very different:

1. When a decision is made after **Consultation,** the decision-maker canvasses the opinions of others but makes the decision. When there is significant, unresolvable disagreement among team members this way of deciding may be a last resort for a team leader. It's ultimately unsatisfactory for team members and for the culture of team because the decision looks like either choosing one set of opinions over another or opting for a personally preferred judgment. Either way, the commitment of group members is likely to be uncertain.

2. **Participation** is a better option. It implies that team members are involved, not only in the discussion about a decision but also in choosing the way that the situation is resolved. However, the final decision may still be left to conventional voting or to a decision by the team leader. Neither of these ways of reaching a decision will necessarily engage the commitment of the whole team.

3. The most engaging way to make team decisions is through full **Collaboration**, aiming to achieve a consensus decision. The whole team is responsible for engaging in the discussion; for deciding on how to resolve differences; and for finding a mutually agreeable resolution. This option often takes the longest time and requires some skill to achieve - BUT, because the aim of consensus is some version of 'we all agree', it is the decision-making process that is most likely to engage the commitment of the whole team.

The diagram below illustrates some of the processes and strategies that may be employed to achieve consensus:

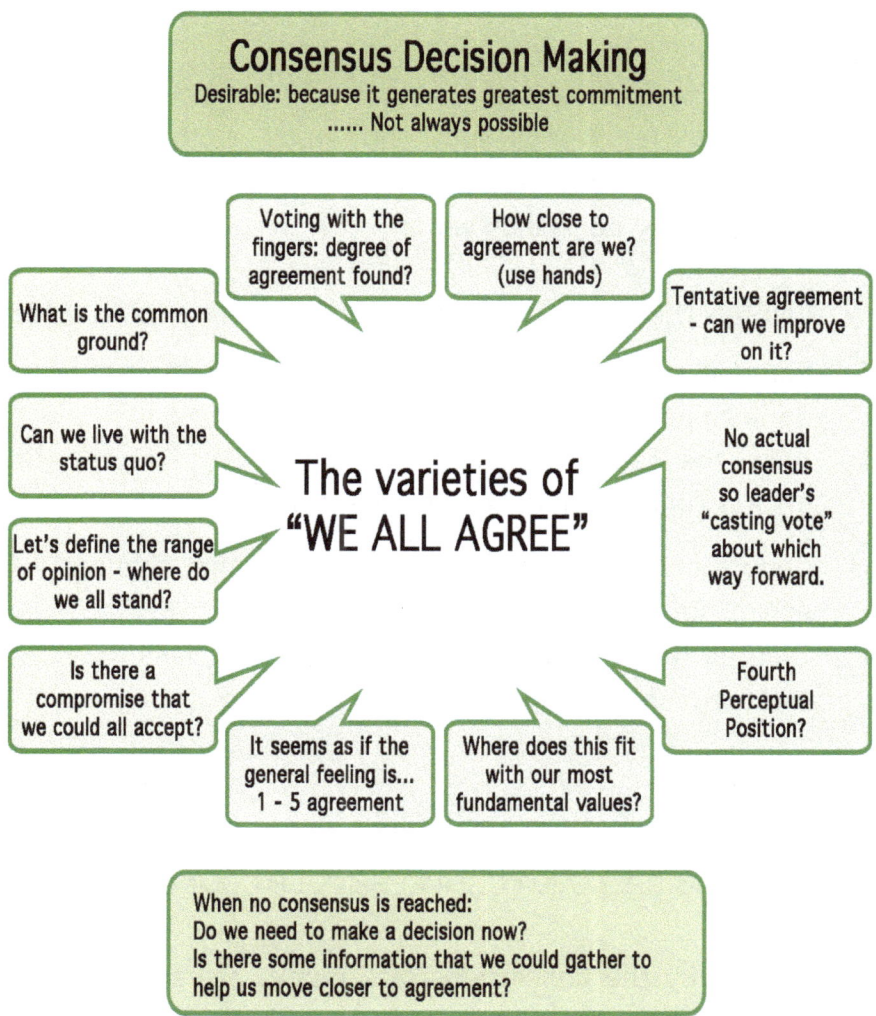

Reaching consensus *may* be as simple as developing an option which every team member agrees with – but it rarely is! More usually, the process used will result in a '*best we can do*' or '*what we can all agree to commit to and take action on*' choice between the variations proposed and discussed.

13.8
USING COACHING QUESTIONS IN DECISION-MAKING

Another very effective process for leading the team towards consensus is the WDEOP process which is the procedure described in the coaching chapter (Chapter 12). This procedure, based on the way our minds work:

W   Clarifies the purpose or goal that the team wants to achiev

D   Reminds team members about what has previously been done to address the issue or problem;

E   Asks the team to evaluate the success of previous efforts (and predict the usefulness of new options);

O   Generates options that will optimise the chances of achieving success;

P   Creates specific, measurable, time-framed plans to which the team are prepared to commit.

13.10
ENCOURAGING OPEN AND COMPREHENSIVE COMMUNICATION

I was struck by the conclusions of a recent piece of research that used technology to track the communication between team members.[2]

What the researchers concluded is that the patterns of communication between members of effective teams are significantly different from those that characterise ineffective teams.

When teams are working well, there is regular face-to-face interaction between most (if not all) team members both within and outside formal meetings. The levels of communication and connection between team members is quite comprehensive – everyone is included. That's quite different from the patterns of less effective teams where the interaction is less frequent, and where there are very weak connections between many team members.

The research does not examine the reasons for the stronger patterns of communication in effective teams, or how these were established and maintained. However, I am fairly certain that I know how it happens. What I also know is that it's never accidental. This habit of frequent and fruitful communication is the usual result when initiating and encouraging trust and mutual respect are priorities for the leader of the team.

This points to the key capacity of successful leaders who need a strong team. They are prepared to invest time to create what they want.

I frequently encounter team leaders who recognise that they need more connection and trust between the members of their team, but they perceive that their team meetings are too busy already.

"I know that my team is a bit cliquey and that some of them don't say much or communicate well with each other", I was recently told by an executive responsible for a senior leadership team. "My problem is that I don't really know what to do about it and I suspect it will take a lot of time – which I don't have."

The issue for this person (and for many others) is that time is at a premium and busy people tend to allocate time according to what they see as immediate priorities. This executive is placing a low value on the connection between team members, chiefly because he does not realise that greater effectiveness would result if he were to make it a priority.

Here's what we know about relationships: people trust those who are predictable, respectful, listen to and value their opinions, have a positive intent and an obvious commitment to a common purpose. They invest the time to talk with and encourage each other when they know that they can contribute to each other's effectiveness and can negotiate in a way that respects difference.

How do we get to develop this level of relationship with our team colleagues?
We spend time talking with them, listening to them, attempting to understand their opinions, learning and using perceptual agility – especially 2nd Perceptual Position

These things cannot, and do not, happen accidentally. They are created purposefully by team leaders who recognise that the ways in which high levels of team communication and trust are developed necessitate the investment of time.

Tuckman's[3] respected model of team formation captures the need for this kind of team member interaction. He posited that

4 phases are required for team to be created successfully: he called them forming, storming, norming and performing:

Formation   Team members meet and get to know each other. They begin the process of exploring each other's ideas and opinions.

Storming   At the point at which differences emerge, conflict is initiated and explored, and team members work out how to disagree agreeably.

Norming   The establishment of team norms, protocols and mutual trust: key to this phase is sufficient conversation to negotiate predictable expectations.

Performing   At this stage, the team operates effectively and collaboratively; learns together, and continuously develops capacity.

While others have refined Tuckman's model, the basis of his insight is sound. It is important to realise though that his 4 phases describe an ongoing journey: the recurrent habits of intra-team communication, rather than a one-time-and-done activity.

Teams change; team members change; individuals within a team learn and develop; new issues emerge. There is a sense in which a team is always forming, returning to storming, and re-norming in order to become relevant to its purpose. The team leader's perceptual awareness is crucial here. She or he must remain alert to the need to re-visit any of Tuckman's phases whenever team performance wilts.

13.11
ENCOURAGING CONSTRUCTIVE DISPUTE AND DEEP THINKING.

The best thinking, the best decisions by a team, need a process of refinement. And, as Patrick Lencioni[4] concludes in his popular treatise on team dysfunction, it's not possible to get the kind of agreement that generates commitment without a willingness to disagree when necessary. In Tuckman's terms, storming almost always precedes performing.

I think of it a bit like the process of turning a dirty piece of rock into an opal. It takes a lot of grinding and polishing to get a sparkling gem. It takes a lot of discussion, contention, frank sharing of opinion and negotiation to create a commitment to which team members will be willingly accountable.

The ability to encourage this kind of creative conflict is central to the creation of real team. It's a high-level capability for leaders. While there is no formula for encouraging and creating a safe space for the frank and ready sharing of opinions, these things create the right environment:
- Modelling by the team leader. When a leader invites disagreement with their own ideas and beliefs, and shows that he respects and listens to contrary opinion with understanding, permission to dissent is given;
- When the leader explains the importance of intra-team conflict - the ways in which the open expression of views and negotiation of disagreement contribute to quality decision-making - team members understand the role of conflict in team performance;
- When the team accepts that their commitment and action are expected, and that they will not be expected to

comfortably commit to team decisions with which they disagree, then conflict is meaningful;
- When it's safe to be a dissenting voice; when no-one is criticised or marginalised for a conflicting or controversial viewpoint; when the search for the best of many options is valued, then dispute is welcomed;
- When everything that is relevant to a decision or plan is expressed in the meeting (i.e. nothing is left to the water cooler or car park) then team members are more likely to be willingly accountable for whatever results.

Encouraging and modelling these things requires determined mind management by the leader, as well as by the team members. Emotions are easily provoked when our strongly held views and trusted beliefs are challenged. As leaders, we often have to call on 2nd, 3rd and 4th Perceptual Positions to stay on our front wheels! It helps us to be deliberately curious about the perceptions and quality pictures in the minds of those who are not in accord with us.

Of all the areas of mental discipline required in leadership, accepting and working through conflict is one of the hardest. Our leadership is usually underpinned by our own passions and personal ideals. It would be so much easier if our colleagues would just go along with us!

The reality though, is that we need far more than simple compliance from our team. What we need if our team and our organisation are to prosper, is the kind of commitment that generates accountability and the determination to follow through and get results. We are reliant on our team to deliver the outcomes that render our leadership effective. There are no short-cuts. To attain effective team functioning, we have to use our own mind-management tools well enough to initiate and encourage disagreement in an agreeable manner.

CHAPTER FOURTEEN

DIRECTION. NOT DIRECTIVES.

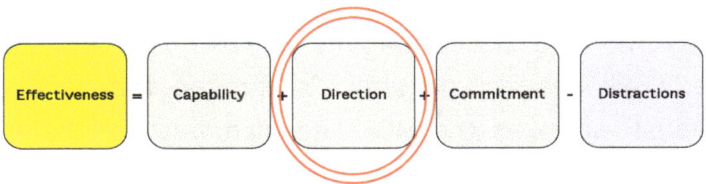

"If you could get all the people in the organisation rowing in the same direction, you could dominate any industry, in any market, against any competition, at any time."

Patrick Lencioni[1]

14.1
KNOWING WHERE TO TAP!

Which way to go? Where best to apply our energy? Where can our skills and capabilities be directed?

I have always been captivated by the urban myth about the elderly plumber who is summoned in desperation when a new, billion-dollar manufacturing plant is brought to a standstill by a hydraulic system that has some kind of mysterious blockage. The old sage wanders around the plant, occasionally putting his ear to a pipe or putting his hand gently on a bend in the system. Finally, he stands for a long time in a distant corner of the building, pulls an ancient pipe wrench from his pocket and taps firmly and decisively on the pipe at that point. There is a gurgling rumble throughout the factory. The blockage is clear. The hydraulics begin to flow as they should. The plumber smiles. He tips his hat and leaves.

The next morning the Managing Director is apoplectic. The plumber's bill has arrived and it's for ten thousand dollars. "Ridiculous!" screams the MD "The man was only here for 20 minutes. Tell him to send an itemised bill so I can see how he justifies that ridiculous fee."

The itemised bill duly arrives. It only has two items on it:
    For tapping on the pipe: $10.00
    For knowing where to tap: $9,990.00

Capability, expertise, experience and skill alone are never enough. They are essentials that only become productive when applied in the right way, at the right time, for the right reason.

For me, 'knowing where to tap' in the story is a metaphor for leading effectively by knowing both where to direct your own capabilities and how to give direction to the efforts of your staff.

Effective leaders know where to tap!

Moreover, they work to ensure that the purpose and practices of their business are so clear to everyone in the company that they too know where to tap!

When we are leaders, it's not enough for us to know where we are going personally. Our job is to build direction into the work of everyone else in the business. Every staff member who is applying their skills in a direction that does not further the purpose of the business is frittering away momentum that could be applied to the organisation's success. Everyone in the organisation who is applying their skills to an activity that will boost performance and productivity is a bonus to the business.

Several years ago, I was introduced to Marco Korn, a Brisbane psychologist[2]. Marco is a deeply insightful thinker, and an expert in applying his knowledge of the mind to workplace situations. The 'Alignment Triangle'© and the 'Conversations for Alignment'© that flow from its use are his creation. His model helps us to understand how to create clarity and agreement in an organisation by focusing on the reasons for actions.

It's commonplace for leaders and managers to give directives to the staff: to tell them not only what has to be done but also how to do it. Their underlying assumption is that the reasons for a particular task or strategy are exclusively executive knowledge. It is presupposed that the workforce simply needs to know what tasks and behaviours are required and be instructed in how to execute those tasks with the greatest efficiency.

In my slightly modified depiction of Marco's alignment triangle (below), we can see that this is identified as the weakest way to provide direction.

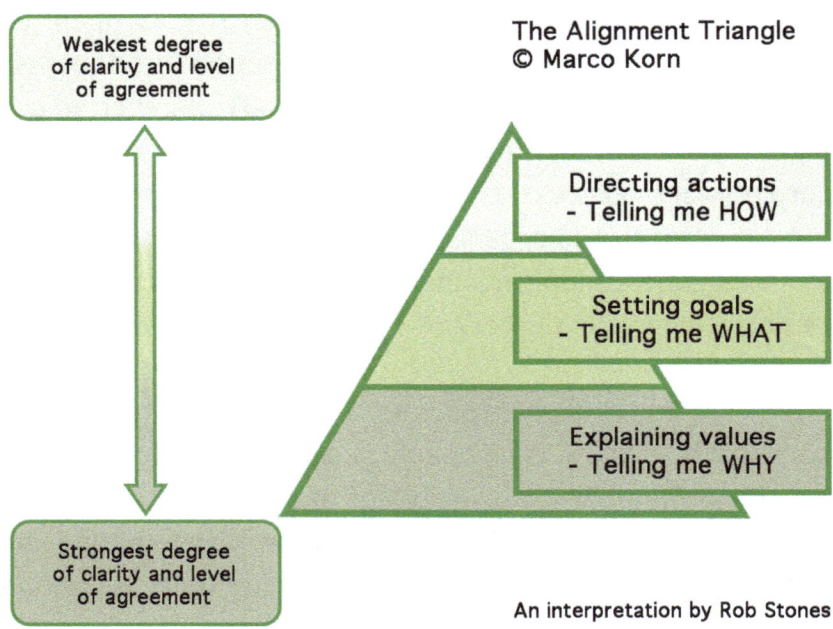

An interpretation by Rob Stones

Providing reasons makes sense when we consider our 'theory of mind' as presented earlier in the book. If our staff are only presented with limited information (what to do and how to do it) then they are left to piece together the why (the rationale) from their own perceptual system and own experience. It's like being told to take steps on a journey and having to guess at the destination – a recipe for confusion and mis-alignment.

If the job is straightforward and everything is going right, then knowing 'WHY' may not always be needed. But when the task is complicated; when the employee is a professional or a skilled worker, there will always be times when it's not clear what to do. These will be the times when knowing 'where to tap' is vital.

When things are not going well, it is crucial to understand the purpose, the explicit business agenda, and the beliefs and values that underpin the company's direction. Knowing WHY is critical.

Understanding the rationale and the intentions behind the company's purpose and direction goes beyond utility. The 'Why' of the organisation creates and fosters the opportunity for initiative and enterprise. Knowing 'Why', every staff member is invited to be a co-designer of the organisation's success. When every individual is encouraged to interpret their own role and tasks through the lens of the company's purpose and strategic intention, then they are liberated to do so in the best way possible. Without an invitation to the conversations that create alignment, individuals are working blind - or left to guess - whenever more than following a directive or policy is required.

Without the discussions that provide clarity and invite commitment, every person in the organisation tends to be governed by their own perceptions of effectiveness and by the value propositions that guide their choices. It is only when 'Conversations for Alignment'© are deliberately initiated and conducted, that the business comes together around one clear direction.

14.2
DIRECTING OUR EFFORTS

In a game of soccer there can be few things more frustrating than scoring skilfully - but in the wrong goal! In life and work nothing is more wasteful than applying ourselves with passion and precision to something that doesn't matter.

As P.F. Drucker[3] puts it: *"There is nothing so useless as doing efficiently that which should not be done at all"*. Capability is undermined if skills and knowledge are directed where they are not needed or will not be effective. It's important for the success of our organisation that we as leaders - and everyone who works alongside us - know what we are doing and why. That we are applying ourselves in the right direction, doing the right thing, in the right way, for the right reason.

Remember that the inevitable motivation of our mind is to behave in whatever ways will (consciously or subconsciously) seem to move us closer to what satisfies us. Identifying what we want and working out how to get it: this is the mainspring of human effort. We naturally want to be safe, powerful and successful: to work towards greater quality of life and an enhanced sense of accomplishment and status. Confidence about our direction, about where we are going and where best to apply our efforts is compelling.

As we noted when examining the SCARF[4] model, the neuroscience of social survival, there are many dimensions of our thinking, emotions and actions which are enhanced by knowing where we are going. As social organisms, humans crave some element of certainty - confidence about where we are going (and why): a sense that our actions are not only personally meaningful but also support our relationships with those around us.

Clear direction can also calm our fears. Whatever we are doing, we tend to weigh risk and reward. Uncertainty and lack of confidence undermine our willingness to devote uninhibited effort to the achievement of purpose. Our survival instinct draws us toward certainty, but it also prompts us to avoid the pain of failure and warns us that we may be vulnerable if we reach too far or aim too high. That's why what we envision must seem attainable; why our intentions and goals must be attractive and realistic.

There are leadership implications from the way the mind deals with aspirational direction. We must balance our business goals with our knowledge that individuals have a need to be personally as well as collectively powerful, and that we are all stubbornly autonomous. If we perceive that the demands of our work restrict our freedoms and limit our capacity for personal achievement, we don't give our best efforts to the enterprise. This is yet another reason why establishing direction is superior to issuing directives – the tone of directives is coercive and impeding; clear direction is empowering and liberating.

The challenge for leaders then is to set the direction of the organisation and frame the accompanying goals somewhat artfully, by balancing lucid and unambiguous future direction with strategic agility so that the business can respond nimbly to changing contexts and demands. The parallel challenge is to set clear direction that is combined with explicit recognition of the autonomy, importance and contribution of all of the workforce whose efforts will be necessary for success. However good the plan, however plain the direction, accomplishment is always dependent on the people in the organisation.

The tool with which to balance all of this complexity is derived from the psychology of human behaviour and is profoundly effective. It is the creation of a 'Window of Certainty'©.

14.3
Shared Direction - The Window of Certainty©

In a publication devoted to this process for establishing direction[5] I wrote this explanation:

'The 'Window of Certainty©' is a framework for leaders and managers who would like to build a culture of powerful alignment in their own complex organisation.

In any enterprise, the 'Window of Certainty©' will provide the architecture for gathering and expressing the unifying intentions and practices that will deepen the commitment and engagement of the workforce. It will embody a shared purpose in which they can have significant buy-in.

'The Window' will enable you to pull together:
- Your vision for the organisation;
- The specific outcomes and products that will be your markers of success;
- The cultural and brand values you espouse;
- The constructive beliefs that will guide your strategies.

THE LEADER-MIND EQUATION

'The Window of Certainty'© collects these four 'frames' in one systematic representation, so that it easily becomes a reference point for the whole organisation."

This way of framing the direction and success formula of an organisation or group was originally devised by Judy Hatswell as the 'Window of Safety' and subsequently developed and modified in the publication *The Window of Certainty*© which we co-authored. We have refined and explored the procedures for creating the 'Window of Certainty'© and shared this approach with hundreds of executives and team leaders. It works! The 'Window' systematically captures the conversations for alignment in the way envisaged by Marco Korn.

There are four frames to the 'Window', each of which contributes a different dimension to the direction and cohesion of an organisation. Each of the frames addresses important questions that every business or institution must consider in its corporate planning:

Our Vision or Purpose:
> *(Where are we going?*
> *What's our explicit improvement agenda?)*

The specific goals or outcomes that relate to the Purpose:
> *(How will we measure success?*
> *What milestones will tell us we are on track?)*

Our beliefs about how to achieve our goals:
> *(What trusted knowledge will guide our strategic practices?)*

The values or branding will we adopt.
> *(What culture will underpin our effectiveness?*
> *What values-in-action define how we do things in this business?)*

The 'Window of Certainty'© provides the balance needed between the organisation and its people. It is a framework that encourages personal autonomy, while anchoring this independence to clear reference points: the vision, values and strategic orientation of the business as a whole.

We know that each individual has personal reference points: the 'Quality World' with which they compare present perceptions. 'The Window of Certainty'© serves as a common 'Quality World' for the organisation; a collaboratively created framework that is the collective reference point for everyone in the school or business.

Although the impetus for creating 'The Window' is often generated by the leader's commitment to provide direction for the organisation, it is always most effective when there is the strongest possible element of co-creation in the development of the framework.

That's why each of the following sections devoted to the frames of 'The Window' include brief suggestions about how to develop it collaboratively.

The principal instrument for creating the 'Window of Certainty'© is conversation. Making time for these 'alignment' conversations and shaping them so that they are productive and move towards consensus, is a constructive leadership skill. The ideas offered below suggest some of the ways in which these discussions might be generated and shaped.

14.4
THE VISION FRAME

Vision describes where we are going; an intended destination. It's an explicit statement of what we want to be achieve.

Think of it like one of those road signposts from an age past (I think we used to call them fingerposts) pointing firmly and clearly down the road to our destination.

From a psychological perspective, a statement of vision (and its creation through an open and transparent process) provides the sense of certainty that calms the fears and doubts generated by our ever-suspicious survival need.

A Vision statement establishes direction. It also provides a point of reference against which to evaluate actions: "If we do this ... will it get us closer to our vision or lead us astray?"

It follows that a statement of vision needs to be clear and to describe a destination state, not the means to get there. It confuses things when beliefs and values are built into the vision. Statements of means and morality belong elsewhere in 'The Window'. These do commonly appear in statements that an organisation makes about itself, but the purpose is very different from the aim of a vision statement. These 'mission statements' are for a client audience. They promote the business. They are often aspirational rather than authentic, and they are not the vision.

It's important that the vision of an organisation is primarily addressed to everyone who works in the organisation. This is where WE are going it says. When we ask every staff member to invest time, energy and commitment in our business, then it's worth the effort to let them know where that investment will take them. Even better if they feel a part of formulating that direction.

We understand, from our exploration of the human mind, that individuals are motivated by their own conceptions of 'Quality'. Making the effort to promote our organisation and its purpose to our staff (our internal clients) pays off when they adopt the business and its vision into their own Quality World.

This is one of the many reasons why vision needs to be both a collaboration and a fairly pragmatic expression of intent. Like every plan for the future, it has to seem possible if it's to engage our energy. While vision does take us beyond the status quo into a preferred future, it has to seem attainable. We are willing to stretch ourselves more readily for something that is just beyond our present grasp, than for a future too amorphous or improbable to induce our enthusiasm.

This the strongest rationale for involving the staff in the formation of the vision. When they have a role in framing the vision, people are likely to find a way of expressing it that means most to them, as well as to the leadership. We are all more likely to identify with a dream of the future that we have a stake in - when we helped to create it rather than being 'told about' it.

Creating the Vision Statement:
Remember that the design parameters of a good vision are:
- Clarity.
- A preferred future (better than what we have now).
- An expression of realistic optimism.

Two possible ways to create an attractive vision are:
1. A Fully Collaborative Process;
2. An opportunity to edit the executive 'draft'.

Both of the above will invite the participation of the workforce; the difference being that a fully collaborative process will start from a blank slate. The 'editing the draft' process will begin with the bones of the vision statement pre-created by the executive or team leader and offered to everyone else for refinement, improvement and variation. Whichever creation process is chosen, as leaders it's valuable when we pay attention to the language that comes back to the leadership group through the collaboration. The words that are significant to our staff are the ones that will help the statement of vision to become meaningful to them.

Leaders can sometimes be wary of a collaboratively developed vision, fearing that the statement may become fragmented by variety of job perspectives within the business. However, engaging the whole staff and inviting them to adopt the wider perspective of leadership, can itself be a reward for using this process. Whenever the contributions of the team miss the wider perspective of the executive leader, this breadth of perspective can be applied sensitively throughout the process. The 'big picture' can be included as a way to shape and to collect the ideas of others, and to help them 'zoom out' to the bigger picture.

Assembling the vision statement collaboratively is based on inviting contributions, and then using group process to meld the contributions into a single statement that adopts the best of all the individual (or group) contributions. Obviously, the smaller your team, the easier this is (and conversely, the larger the team, the more work is involved).

When this process is adopted, we want to tap into the highest possible aspiration of our people. Because corporate cynicism is a real but unfortunate presence within the ranks in many organisations, it's important to ask the questions that encourage optimism and enlightened self-interest, and which avoid mutual pessimism.

Questions such as:
- "Ideally, where will this organisation be 5 years from now?"
- "Imagine that you are describing the state of our business in 5 years: What would you like to be saying about it?"
- "If the organisation were really thriving in 5 years' time, and you were proud to be part of the changes we have made, how would you describe us?"

The answers to these questions can be fed into processing groups who will refine them, exctract the essence from them, and feed them back to the staff for comment.

This last step (feeding back the synthesised statement) is important. Because we are aiming for statements of vision that are succinct, few people will see their actual contribution in the final draft. But if we ask: "Is the sense of what you contributed captured in the statement?", then we invite them to recognise and appreciate, the inclusion of their key ideas.

14.5

The Outcomes Frame

Specific and measurable **Outcomes** enhance the clarity of the vision statement. They identify the elements of the improvement agenda that show us that we have achieved (or are on the way to achieving) the vision.

In the Outcomes frame, we spell out the measurable differences between the 'now' and the future we are creating. Outcomes help to define the purpose in such a way that progress can be observed and measured.

Outcomes can be short-term or long-term, describing either the quality of our products; the results we will achieve when our vision becomes reality; or the interim milestones through which we will measure our progress towards our longer-term goals.

Without well-defined and measurable outcomes, even the clearest statement of vision can lack the specificity required. When the outcomes associated with the vision are elucidated, the organisation can measure its march towards success.

In a large organisation, different departments or teams may

specify the outcomes that will demonstrate the particular contribution that the sector will make to the achievement of the vision. In smaller businesses, one set of outcomes will usually be enough.

Creating the Outcomes Frame

As with the Vision Frame, inviting widespread contributions to the formation of the outcomes Frame are welcomed. To some extent, the diversity of work tasks in the organisation will determine the number and variety of outcome statements needed. However, trying to track and measure a large number of outcomes can not only create confusion, but can also become another 'job' that has to be done that does not contribute directly to the organisation's productivity.

A word about data: outcomes are often measured in numbers – and hence are displayed as data. So, whether we are measuring the profitability of a company; the number of new clients; the results achieved by students or the volume of product; we use numbers and graphs to track our improvement. Measuring outcomes is a data-rich activity. However, data can be a trap that is often not only misleading, but also distracting. Allocating time and energy to measuring, tracking and reporting on data does not itself help us to achieve better outcomes – so we should be cautious about investing the time and energy that could be otherwise used to learn and implement productive strategies.

So, the design parameters for creating the Outcomes frame are:
- Identify concrete and measurable 'products' that will clarify elements of the vision.

- Select outcomes that to help narrow and focus the business's purpose and productivity.
- Ensure that the outcomes measured provide feedback on the effectiveness of the business's journey towards its goals.
- Limit the number of outcomes selected so that there are as many as needed to track the key improvements needed,++ but no more

Questions that we can ask to elicit outcomes are:

- "How will we know that we are improving and making progress towards achieving our vision?"
- "As we work towards the achievement of our vision, how will we measure our progress?"
- "What would be a cause for celebration?"

Useful outcomes are always verifiable. If an outcome statement is too general to be tested or has so long a timeline that the relationship to the activity of the business seems tenuous, then it fails the test of usefulness. It will not sufficiently narrow and focus the improvement agenda of the business.

As a rule, if an outcome cannot be evaluated then it is not precise enough to be used. A business without tangible outcomes can never 'fail', but it can't 'succeed' either!

That does not mean that businesses can only limit themselves to outcomes that can be measured numerically. Nor does it mean that every outcome area *should* be measured.

A well-balanced approach would be to choose and benchmark a variety of the indicators that are likely to show that the vision and purpose of the business are being achieved, and then persevere with those indicators.

Once a list of possible outcomes is collaboratively generated, they can be refined and collated either by the leadership group or by a group that represents diverse perspectives within the organisation.

To generate widespread ownership of the outcomes it's important to complete the process by presenting the collated statement of outcomes back to the whole staff for comment, adoption or further refinement.

14.6
THE BELIEFS FRAME

Beliefs are our ideas about how things work. They guide our strategies because they are our trusted perceptions of the world - what we accept as 'true in our experience'.

Remember that everyone accumulates knowledge as they learn and grow, and beliefs form that special category of our accumulated knowing: understandings that guide us as we try to work out how to be successful and happy in the world. As we noted in Section Two, we treat beliefs as if they are true (often not only for us but for everyone). But beliefs only *seem* like truths. We attach emotional certainty to them because our experience has taught us that they benefit us. It is need-satisfying to act as though the belief is true.

Whatever their validity, we do rely on and trust those perceptions that we have adopted as beliefs. However, honest reflection will soon suggest to us that our beliefs are not infallible. All of us can think of things we have believed, but no longer do. We leave the beliefs of childhood behind relatively easily (though sometimes regretfully). Many of us believed that matter is solid until faced by the new science that tells us that everything is created from the dynamic relationships between sub-atomic particles that are themselves not even visible until they are in relationship with other particles.[6]

The point is that because beliefs are created from knowledge, when we have new knowledge (or a means to evaluate our present knowledge) beliefs change. As we elicit the shared beliefs that create this frame, the criterion upon which to make our choice should be **usefulness**.

When a group of people working together doesn't articulate or share their beliefs, they may find it difficult to understand why they disagree about the best way to achieve the outcomes they have identified. They may not identify beliefs as the source of these different pathways to success, so productive cohesion becomes problematic. However, when there is explicit sharing of beliefs, the reasons for preferring different approaches become clear – the beliefs are different!

When this kind of disagreement emerges, the test of **usefulness** is the way to resolve or collapse most differences – i.e. which of these beliefs will be most useful to us in striving to achieve our purpose?

In developing the Beliefs Frame, these aspects of the process contribute to team cohesion:

1. People take the time and effort to think through the beliefs that they hold and share these with other people. The field is narrowed because participating staff are asked to focus on their work-related beliefs: the beliefs they hold which are related to the achievement of the goals that have been identified in the Outcomes Frame. This step alone is powerful. When beliefs are shared - and individuals realise that their colleagues have the same belief - they feel affirmed. When they discover that respected colleagues have different beliefs, they are more likely to question their own intuitive presuppositions.
2. Groups are asked to evaluate all of the beliefs presented against the standard of **usefulness.** This is an unusual comparison in this context (though we know from our theory of mind that it is the relevant one). Using useful/un-useful as a basis for evaluation moves the conversation in a pragmatic direction.
3. As agreement is reached about which beliefs are most useful, we can use these as a basis for agreeing on the strategies (the courses of action) that are most likely to be effective. As Dilts[5] has commented, the beliefs we are most affected by typically are the ones we are least conscious of. By eliciting common beliefs, we are in concordance - consciously accepting the implications of the beliefs we have in common.

Although I have commented on the uniqueness of perceptions, because beliefs are generalisations, they are often readily accepted by people working in a common enterprise. We all have many beliefs in common with other colleagues. A society or a workplace would not operate well without these commonalities.

Shared beliefs can be useful and can support our survival and success. Just think how dangerous it would be to drive on a motorway if everyone had different beliefs about safe driving!

The other significant thing about working with the Beliefs Frame is that beliefs change. Your beliefs will have changed over time. They will almost certainly change again in the future, because beliefs are not immutable. They change when experience and new knowledge contradict them. They change when we realise that they no longer serve us.

One of the reasons for taking the time for the deep conversations that create the Beliefs Frame is that the knowledge and shared experience that create this frame will change (or at least modify) some un-useful beliefs.

Developing the Beliefs Frame

Because our different repertoires of belief lead to very different intuitive assumptions about effective practice, the Beliefs Frame is critical for unifying direction. Consequently, this frame of the 'Window' is often the longest conversation and the most likely to be ongoing, but it is also the most powerful source of employee alignment.

When everyone in the business agrees on what is needed to

maintain quality, or what practices will be most effective in assembling the product, then they will adopt common strategies and methods.

When embedded in the context of collegial conversation the questions that can be most helpful are:
- "What do we believe will guide effective practice?" or "In what ways do we believe we can achieve the levels of productivity and the quality of outcomes we intend?"

Step by Step
- The first step is always to ask individuals to consider and write down their own beliefs. Remember: these are the beliefs they have that are related to the success of the organisation and the achievement of the target outcomes.
- Then share individual belief statements in small groups. The group is asked to be curious about these individual beliefs, especially when differences emerge.
- The groups ask each other about each belief: "Will the strategies suggested by that belief help us to achieve our purpose – or hinder us?) On this basis the group identifies its 10 most useful beliefs. These key beliefs from each group are displayed.
- A process is put in place for the output for all groups to be synthesised. The larger the staff group the more complex and thorough this process will need to be. (In a group of up to 100, I use a process where [after the outputs are put into alike groups] every individual allocates up to 10 'sticker dots' to the beliefs they regard as most important for the organisation's success.

This makes it comparatively easy to synthesise many beliefs – just count the dots!)
- As with the other frames, the statement of key beliefs created by the process is fed back to the whole staff - with an opportunity for them to provide feedback and to refine the statement.

14.7

THE VALUES FRAME – 'VALUES IN ACTION'

Values, in this context, are the critical foundation of both culture and branding: both 'This is the way we do things around here' and 'this is what we stand for'.

There is a distinction between these values-in-action and more theoretical principles. For example, many people will intuitively agree that they value 'service' or 'respect', but without discussion and consensus this value is enacted in many different ways - depending on personal interpretation and perspective.

The focus of the Values Frame is to generate discussion about the values that underpin the organisational culture which will help our business to thrive. This discussion will focus heavily on the specific behaviours associated with each value, in order to remove the ambiguity that is common in values-laden language.

Most values are commonly expressed as nominalisations: a way of turning a verb into a noun; a behaviour into a name. The name can stand for many different behaviours and because of this we often have very different pictures in our head even when we say we share the same value.

When we ask people to identify their values, we often hear them expressed as names like these: respect, trust, kindness, honesty, generosity, service, responsibility. Each of these naming words can be unpacked into many different behaviours. Expressed as behaviours, 'Respect', 'Trust' and 'Kindness' might refer to:

- Respecting (which might mean showing consideration, accepting others' ideas, showing politeness, or treating others with unconditional positive regard);
- Trusting or being trustworthy (with meanings that include being predictable, sincere, loyal or reliable, thoughtful of others);
- Being kind (among many behaviours could mean showing compassion, nurturing others, behaving in a caring way or paying attention to people).

As you can see, there are many possible variations of what the 'name' of the value might mean in practice. The Values Frame of the window serves its purpose best when the name of the value is unpacked sufficiently so that every person can clearly understand what the value-in-action will look like, sound like and feel like.

For example: I worked with a group of middle level managers who all agreed that they valued 'collegiality' and 'mutual respect'. These were values established by a former CEO and they were adopted unreflectively. Pressed about the importance of these values, they said that they were very important in relation to the way they treated each other. However, in private conversation, several told me that there was a culture of mistrust in the organisation and that the chief advantage of the values was that they constrained the managers from open conflict!

The heart of the problem was that the behaviours they associated with 'collegiality' and 'mutual respect' included 'being congenial and affable: getting along with each other at all costs; showing good humour; always being polite; avoiding controversy and never openly disagreeing'.

The 'values' they all appeared to subscribe to, were not supporting what they wanted and needed. They would have been better served by frank and open dialogue leading to mutual understanding of each other's work. When (with my encouragement) they shared what they thought the present values meant, they soon saw that all of the misunderstanding and mistrust they experienced arose directly from the lack of discussion about what kind of culture they needed to be effective, and what valued behaviours would create that culture. They quickly abandoned the values statement they had inherited and decided that more useful values were honesty (always telling each other the truth about their motives and priorities), curiosity (always attempting to understand other points of view and job priorities), being trustworthy (showing they could be relied upon to support each other, follow through on promises and acting in predictable ways) and willingness to be courteous and agreeable when disagreeing with each other.

The questions you might pose for the Values Frame could be:

- "What values should underpin the way we work and interact with each other (and with our clients)?"
- "What are the values-in-action or valued behaviours that will be most likely to help us to work together in achieving our purpose?"
- What values-in-action will underpin the behaviours we choose to build our culture of success?"

Exploring the Values Frame

Remember that the benefits that arise from discussing the Values Frame are:

1. To determine the cultural values to which each staff member ascribes importance. These are the descriptions of the way we will treat each other on the journey to our shared destination: the values-in-action that individuals believe should be adopted across the organisation.
2. To unpack these values as values-in-action. What behaviours will result from these values if they are universally adopted in our business? What will we see each other doing or hear each other saying?
3. To decide which of the behaviours discussed will contribute the most to a culture of success in the organisation.
4. To adopt values-in-action that are well-understood and supported.

As we saw with the Beliefs Frame, the Values Frame is most likely to come together after small group discussion is used for steps 1 & 2 above. All responses are then collated and then all the values-in-action that are significant across the groups are subsequently fed back to the staff to be prioritised at step 3.

The completed Values Frame will include all the values that attract high levels of consensus. Because these are all focused on the way in which people speak and act, the result will be a resilient workplace culture in which individuals will thrive and be prepared to do their best.

14.8

THE WINDOW OF CERTAINTY ENCOURAGES AUTONOMY

The 'Window of Certainty'© invites the creative autonomy of every individual in the organisation. Unlike a more traditional 'code of conduct' or norms-based approach, there are no 'rules'. The four frames of the 'Window' create boundaries for acceptable behaviours, but within these boundaries there is a wealth of personal freedom. By implication, ***everything*** is encouraged that:

- Leads to the achievement of the vision;
- Contributes to the identified outcomes;
- Is aligned with the beliefs and values of the organisation.

That provides lots of freedom!

As we will see in the 'Commitment' sections of this book, high degrees of personal autonomy are a pre-requisite for commitment and engagement. Because the 'Window' approach only defines the boundaries which frame the common direction of the business, it encourages the free reign of individuality within these boundaries. The frames of the 'Window' create coherence and certainty without proscribing individual differences and approaches. Many choices exist within the 'Window' and personal creativity and individual preference contribute to the advance of workplace effectiveness.

14.9
THE LEADER AS BOUNDARY-RIDER

Setting up norms for the organisation using the 'Window of Certainty'© implies a clear role for the leadership of the business – the necessity to be the guardian of the agreed boundaries.

The key to the effectiveness of the 'Window of Certainty'© approach is that it presupposes and encourages autonomy. It recognises that personal freedom is a necessary condition for personal achievement. Similarly, the respect for individual difference which supports personal freedom spawns the kinds of relationships that create a culture of effectiveness. These are the three pillars of an effective direction for any organisation: autonomy, individual achievement and respectful relationships.

The complication that comes with encouraging autonomy in this way is the very human tendency to explore limits.

All of us who have raised, or taught children know that they usually push against the boundaries we impose. They test them to see if they are real, how universally they apply, when they can be ignored and when they can't.

The 'child' in us that once tested the limits of our youthful freedoms is the parent to the adult we become. When a boundary or a limit is imposed on us at any age, those perimeters will (sooner or later) be tested. When autonomy is encouraged, individuals will explore its frontiers.

The job of the leader then, is to ensure that the boundaries remain clear, that the limits are understood; that those who test the demarcation lines between responsible behaviour and the 'step-too-far' are gently but firmly reminded where the boundary is drawn.

Without the leader's willingness to patrol the boundaries created by 'The Window', the frames become blurred and the cohesion created by the process is lost. By demonstrating their commitment to honouring the norms created through 'The Window' process, leaders deliver certainty and safety to the members of our work force. Without a boundary-rider, the boundaries sag sadly towards disregard.

14.10
THE BOUNDARY CONVERSATION

The instrument through which the frames of the 'Window of Certainty'© are maintained and illuminated is a conversation. It's a firm conversation with a simple structure. It contains no intention to reprimand or criticise. It is focused on values and beliefs, not behaviours. When its purpose is complete, the boundary is clarified, and commitment is restored. An effective boundaries conversation can be enlightening and encouraging. Even when areas of disagreement are revealed, maintaining a positive future frame almost always pays off.

The steps of the Boundary Conversation are these:
1. We notice a breach in the boundary (the issue or incident) and initiate a conversation;
2. We explain our role (boundary rider);
3. We avoid putting the accent on the behaviour that concerns us: only the value beliefs or outcomes that are involved. We may have to 'flip' ourselves to do this. It is crucial to focus on what we want, NOT what we don't want;
4. We ask about what this 'value' means to the team member;
5. At this point the conversation will go in one of two different directions:
    a. There will be agreement about the importance of the value and some positive discussion about how to be inside the boundary.

     or
- b. There will be different views about the value under discussion and the leader will be assertive in their boundary-rider role. The leader's responsibility is to coach the staff member toward greater alignment with the values of the business.
6. Agreement is reached about the future. We thank the other person.

The example conversation that follows was initiated by a sales manager following a second customer complaint about late delivery of a product. Follow the conversation with the structure above in mind.

The manager invites Robert to join him at a neutral venue so that they can have a chat. With coffees in front of them, the Sales Manager begins:

SM	"I want to sound you out about the things that you see as important to us in attracting and retaining customers."
Robert	"Well"…. (*Pause*) "It's important, of course."
SM	"So, in that context, what do you think are the most important things about our client service?"
Robert	(*Thinks he knows what this is about*) "Is this about Mr Evans getting his printing late?"
SM	"I do know about that. But I don't want to talk about that in particular. I am more interested in what you think about client service in general. What does our claim to offer 'exceptional client service' mean to you?"

Robert   "I suppose it means that we will look after our customers better than anyone else - better than our competitors..... Look, I know that I was a bit slack with Mr Evans' order."

SM   "Thanks for recognising that there was a problem there. But we can't change what is past, so I don't want to dwell on that. I am more interested on what 'exceptional customer service' means to you as a key person in our sales team? What does it mean for you going forward?"

Robert   "I won't be slack in the future!"

SM   "Robert, I am not sitting here to blame you, or complain about something that's happened. But I do genuinely think it's important to make sure that we are on the same page with regard to the way we look after our clients. What do you think 'exceptional customer service means?"

Robert   "I hadn't thought about it that much....."

(The SM waits and lets the silence do the heavy lifting.)

Robert   "I suppose that our service to clients will only really be exceptional if they can absolutely trust us not to let them down ... to make sure that they get exactly what they want .... even get it early. And if anything is holding up the supply chain, to do everything that we can to get things moving, and let the customer know what's happening."

SM   *(Paraphrases what he has heard)* "That sounds good to me: give customers what they want, when they want it or earlier, chase things up if there are hold-ups and keep the customer in the loop. Anything else?"

Robert	"Maybe anticipate what they may want next ... and be really friendly and supportive. Listen to their problems when they grumble to us. Mr Evans does go on a bit at times."
SM	"He can be trying. But I agree with you. Part of our job is to listen and be empathic so that clients know we care. It sounds as if we both agree about what we mean by exceptional client service."
Robert	"I think we do."
SM	"What does this mean for you in the future?"
Robert	"I think I am on board with most of it. But I should try to deliver early rather than on time .. get on to our suppliers as soon as we have an order. I know that there are a couple of wholesalers who are always slow. I think I should anticipate that and keep checking". *(Pauses)* "I should contact Mr Evans and apologise. I haven't done that yet."
SM	"I think he would appreciate hearing from you. When will you do that?"
Robert	"I can do it today. I will give him a call later this morning".
SM	"And with regard to suppliers who are often slow, can you bring that issue up at our next sales team meeting? If we are all having problems with the same sources, we could look for alternatives."
Robert	"I can do that. It will be good to talk it through with the team."
SM	"Thanks Robert. I am glad we had this talk."

Now you might observe that Robert was cooperative. My experience is that most people are when they realise that blame is off the table. However, how would the sales manager continue the conversation if Robert were less responsive? Let's go back to the same conversation at the point where the sales manager asks what 'exceptional customer service' means.

Robert	"It doesn't mean much really, it's just a slogan. Most businesses say something like that. I think I work about as hard as most people to keep customers happy."
SM	"You have not been attaching much significance to our claim to provide exceptional service? And, if I understand you, you feel that you work about as hard as can be expected?"
Robert	"That's about it. And Mr Evans sure is a difficult customer to keep happy. His expectations are way unreasonable!"
SM	"You think that good service means only keeping our customers happy if they are easy to work with?"
Robert	"I didn't mean that exactly. Surely you agree that some people are hard to keep happy?"
SM	"I do agree about that. *(Pauses)* Robert, I am very pleased that we are having this conversation because it seems that there may be a few differences between the way that you are thinking about client service and the importance which the company attaches to it. In this organisation, we really do want to offer a better quality of service to our clients - different

from whatever they might experience somewhere else.

Our reasoning is that most people will take their business to where they feel most looked after. If we tell them that we offer exceptional service - and they find out that we do really care about our customers - then it's likely that they will be loyal to us. Do you think that's important in a business with lots of competitors?"

Robert	"I suppose so. I wasn't thinking about that."
SM	"What are the alternatives?"
Robert	"You mean, if we don't look after them, they will go to someone else."
SM	"Does that matter to you?"
Robert	"If the business doesn't do well, maybe I will not have a job?"
SM	"Investing in the company's values might mean investing in you. Is that a way of seeing things?"
Robert	"Yes."
SM	"Worth looking after a grumpy client for?"
Robert	(*Long pause*) "Perhaps I should call Mr Evans and apologise…?"
SM	"I think he would appreciate hearing from you. When will you do that?"

When we have a 'boundary rider' conversation with a colleague, the aim is always positive: to encourage them back inside the boundaries. When we create our 'Window of Certainty'© for the organisation, it provides a value-based, reasoned structure to which we can refer when talking with staff. Because of the framework, working in the interests of the business is never a managerial whim. It's always about achieving clarity about why we do things.

There are a couple of caveats that accompany this type of conversation:
- The 'Window' really must be about the boundaries: within those boundaries there must be genuine autonomy.
- The conversation must be future solution-focused and contain no hint of blame. When people feel that they are being blamed their energy is always focused on justifying what they did.

14.11
THERE MUST BE A BOTTOM LINE!

I don't mean to imply that a 'boundary conversation' will always be successful. That would be totally unrealistic. Like every other leader, I have encountered staff members who refuse to remain inside the boundaries, despite the best efforts of their leaders.

In almost every organisation there will be (from time to time) employees for whom employment is an inconvenient interruption in their life: those who will rarely accept personal responsibility, and even those who get some kind of private joy from sabotaging the efforts of the business and the work of their colleagues. Not everybody has quality pictures that are noble or responsible!

When we have to deal with people such as these, I believe that as leaders we are best served by taking a three-step approach:

Step 1: Am I the problem? Is there something in the way that I, or my executive colleagues, are leading and managing this person that is contributing to their indifference or resistance?
'Looking in the mirror' is always step 1. It is an expression of our commitment to take personal responsibility. If there is something that we can improve in order to engage and include the person that we see as a problem, we should do it!

Step 2: If we can't see how to improve what **we** are doing, then step 2 is to ask ourselves if the person we are concerned about is functioning at an acceptable compliance level. They may not be doing a great job: we may wish that they would be more productive and responsive - but if they are doing as directed and working to the level which is compatible with their terms of employment then we may have to accept that they are here to stay! If this is the case, our best course of action is to go back to the mirror and ask ourselves and our senior colleagues: "What can we do to increase this team member's level of engagement in order for them to be more productive?" If we can think of any way to increase their engagement and productivity by a few % points (without disproportionate time and effort) we should do so.

Step 3: If the person concerned is operating outside one of the frames of our 'Window of Certainty'©; and if their work ethic and output is damaging the productivity of the organisation, or undermining the commitment of their colleagues, then it is unlikely that they are working at even a compliance level. The processes for dismissing them may be difficult and tedious, but it is our job as boundary-riders to ensure that the boundaries are applied.

I have found that, in the few cases where I had to pursue the processes for dismissal because of diminished or inadequate performance, the response of the person's workplace colleagues was relief. The question I was mostly asked was: "What took you so long? – we don't understand why this person was not dismissed long ago!"

Damaging underperformance is most visible to - and has the greatest impact on - the team members who have to work harder because they perceive that one person is not pulling their weight. There are few things more dispiriting than working with energy and initiative alongside a colleague who is eroding your enthusiasm and abilities by their apparent laxity.

Ensuring that there is a bottom line – i.e. a level of under-performance and lack of commitment that is totally unacceptable - is one of the most unpleasant but necessary responsibilities of the leader as boundary-rider!

Chapter Fifteen

Commitment

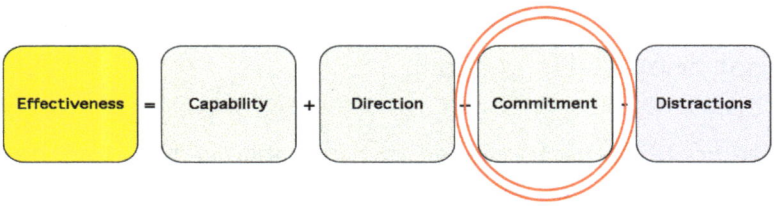

"Today, no leader can afford to be indifferent to the challenge of engaging employees in the work of creating the future. Engagement may have been optional in the past, but it's pretty much the whole game today."

Gary Hamel[1]

15.1
Where Commitment Fits

Just the other day, I was talking with a group of middle level leaders about the '*Leader-Mind* Formula'. In particular we were considering a question one of them had asked: a query about the relative importance of the three positive variables

(Capability + Direction + Commitment) that combine in effective performance. I was not contributing much apart from questions (always the best way to learn), but one person had a lot to say.

Daniel is a former AFL player who played at close to the highest level of the game. His perspective was very clear: "Look at it as if we were talking about a football team" he said.

"Capability is the skill variable; no one can compete at a high level unless they can show skill under pressure. Direction is about knowing where to put your effort - how the game works and where to direct your energy to make the most difference. It's game nous. It's knowing the team's plan and your part in it. Commitment is the motivation variable. It's the effort, energy, the 'run until you drop and then keep on running' factor."

We were listening. His metaphor seemed to work.

"The thing is", Daniel continued, "there is no point in asking which is most important out of capability, direction and commitment. No team or individual can succeed without all three. All the knowledge and effort in the world will come to nothing without skill. A player with skill and experience but who contributes less than 100% is going to let you down. A player with individual skill who tries incredibly hard but has no game nous will not be in the right position when it counts. In sport as in leadership", he continued, "all three are needed if individuals are going to be effective and the team is going to be successful."

The group thought about this for a while, and then one of the other members of the training group observed: "They are all inter-dependent really. If commitment grows, then individuals will willingly learn new skills and be more focused on the goals of the business, and so on."

15.2
FROM DISENGAGED TO COMMITTED.

I know what being uncommitted at work feels like. As a young man, working to support himself during the college holidays, I endured a series of jobs that had for me a zero level of engagement. On the production line in a chicken processing plant, the hours passed with agonising slowness. The cement warehouse and the wine bottling plant were much the same (except that loading bags of ready-mix cement was also physically exhausting). I was a warm, barely upright body filling a gap in the vacancies column. I was not the slightest bit interested or engaged in the work I was doing. I watched the clock all day. I did as little as possible. I came to work only for the money.

In a challenging speech that I was able to access through YouTube many years ago, Dr Gary Hamel[2] described that level of commitment as 'showing up'. It's not a level of energy and commitment that will help businesses to thrive - even those few that require unskilled manual labour - and that kind of work is increasingly rare.

We are now firmly in the era of what Peter Drucker[3] described as 'knowledge workers'. In almost every organisation, the knowledge and skill that support productivity and profit are supported by the training and proficiency of the workforce. Increasingly, businesses are the domain of qualified professionals or highly skilled technicians. The success of the organisation that employs them depends on their training and skill.

Knowledge workers thrive on the ability to be individually effective and tend to lose interest when applying someone else's solution. They crave the autonomy that allows them to demonstrate their personal knowledge and proficiency[4].

The question for leaders - whose teams largely consist of professional or skilled staff - is: "How do we minimise 'showing up' and maximise 'whatever it takes to succeed?'"

In the address referred to above, Gary Hamel offered his audience a way of thinking about the importance of paying attention to the commitment of our workforce, together with the leader behaviours that encourage different levels of engagement and performance energy.

The table below is my adaptation of Hamel's hierarchy of commitment and accomplishment:

Showing up	Coming to work.
Compliance	Performing to the minimum standard expected on required tasks.
Conformity:	Doing what's expected in the expected way to fit in with your colleagues.

Diligence: Working hard at the tasks you are given to do within the boundaries of present knowledge and skill.

Responsibility: Accepting personal accountability for quality performance - including willingness to learn new skills when required.

Initiative: Independently working towards the achievement of outcomes through self-generated learning.

Enterprise: Actively seeking to improve quality and showing resourceful leadership in creating new paradigms of quality.

The questions generated by Hamel's analysis are: "What level of commitment and capability will sustain and improve your organisation?" and "What are the leader behaviours which are most likely to encourage the levels of engagement that you want?"

Notice that there are two presuppositions in Hamel's hierarchy and the questions posed above:
- The assumption that higher levels of commitment include learning and the growth of capability. This echoes the conclusion reached by the members of the aforementioned training group: that the elements of effectiveness and productivity are all inter-related.
- That there are leadership behaviours that are likely to encourage and nurture high levels of commitment; and conversely there are those that will inhibit effortful participation.

This chapter is mostly devoted to the ways in which we as leaders, can energise and support our team members so that their commitment and capability are enhanced. We will examine what we know that will support energetic engagement - as well as what will deter it! In the spirit of the self-evaluation theme that runs strongly though the pages of this book, we will also apply this to ourselves. If we lead in ways that support and hone the elements of our own commitment, we will be increasingly effective. As we consider the ways in which energy and enthusiasm are enhanced by thoughtful leaders, we can reflect on what we are doing to stoke the fires of our own vigorous contribution to the organisation.

Using Hamel's hierarchy as a guide we can ask ourselves: "What level of commitment can we insist on? Is there a level of contribution we can mandate?

As soon as we look at his analysis through these eyes, we can see clearly that we can't *command* enterprise and initiative. These represent gifts of human creativity that have to be freely given. We can't really direct people to work diligently or take personal responsibility for outcomes; we can only specify minimum levels of accountability in that regard. We can't even require conformity: each team member will work out for themselves what behaviours will 'fit in' with their colleagues. What we are left with is compliance: the lowest level of commitment! While we can (if we choose to) use threats and rewards to pressure staff to come to work and do as they are told, this strategy will result in the lowest level of motivation. Anything more that they contribute will depend on whether they see it in their own interests to do so!

15.3
THE REAL MOTIVES OF HUMAN BEHAVIOUR

You will notice that all of the above is at odds with the widely held idea that leaders can and should 'motivate' their people. Talk about motivating others is embedded in the common parlance, but it's misleading because it's mistaken.

We are all motivated internally, from the inside – not from outside. The generators - the motives of our behaviours - come from our internal processing and from our individual striving to gratify our genetic needs. We compare what we want with what we perceive to be happening and then behave in ways that will increase our satisfaction levels - or lessen our frustration.

As we observed in Section Two, the basis of internal motivation is the gratification of our own genetic needs: the needs for achievement, autonomy, relatedness, learning and self-sustaining behaviours (survival).

These intrinsic motives are the source of our energetic participation. When we have a sense of personal achievement; when we are enjoying learning, extending ourselves and acquiring new competences; when we are encouraged by stimulating and supportive relationships; when we have enough independence to promote our individual creativity and initiative; when we feel safe and certain about the purpose of our work - when these things come together we thrive!

The reverse - the conditions of disengagement - starkly illustrate the importance of need-satisfaction at work. If our work is consistently boring; if we are expected to follow a script without variation; if there is little opportunity for personal achievement; if we perceive the imposed expectations as threatening - in these circumstances we lose energy swiftly!

What this means is that it is the leader's job to create the conditions in which intrinsic motivation is able to thrive. And if we have senior staff and HR professionals who are attempting to impose external controls that we know will crush willing engagement, it's our job to challenge those methods. We can't 'motivate' anyone, but we can make it more or less likely that they will be self-motivated: in the work conditions we create; the kind of contribution we encourage; and by the culture that we shape and inspire through our own behaviours.

15.4
MISCONCEPTIONS ABOUT MOTIVATION

Unfortunately, leaders who do think it is their job to 'motivate' their team members usually end up with the opposite of what they want. This kind of thinking implies that there are things that can be done to people, or for people, that will increase their energy and engagement.

Leaders who are beguiled by this ideology spend energy and money devising ways to reward or bribe their colleagues into working harder - think bonuses, awards, 'employee of the month' or the subtle use of promotional 'opportunity'. These leaders may use actual or implied threats or other 'punishing' strategies to coerce staff members into working harder - withholding bonuses, excluding them from opportunities or marginalising individuals are commonplace). An even more ineffectual version of these attempts to control the efforts and commitment of staff is the motivational talk, or harangue. All of these are misguided efforts to control other individuals. The awful thing is that they are bound to misfire. Controlling conditions are rarely need-satisfying; they erode autonomy and usually damage relationships. By defining achievement as 'deserving of a bonus', they create a 'bosses know best' environment in which individual perception of achievement is not valued and the kind of learning people do is imposed.

By attempting to invent external controls to raise the levels of zealous participation, command and control leaders impose conditions that have the opposite effect. From inside the external control paradigm it seems logical to try to 'make' people do things. But if we go back to Hamel's hierarchy of commitment, we can easily see what the result will be. Because the only level of commitment that we can insist on is compliance, that's all we can be certain of achieving. Those who are already uncommitted will respond with obedience and minimum contribution. They will work to rule. Those who enter the workplace with high levels of intrinsic motivation will have that eroded and become discouraged by the controlling environment.

It's such a waste of potential. It's wasteful because influencing the level of internal motivation of our staff is eminently attainable. We can create the conditions in which the powerful internal motivators of our team members will be liberated. We can, and should, create and influence the context and culture, the language and expectation, the social dynamic and sense of meaning that pervades our organisation.

We've already noted the general point that, when the work environment allows people to satisfy their own cognitive and survival needs, intrinsic motivation is given the opportunity to work in the service of the organisation. Beyond that we can look at the specific benefits of encouraging responsible autonomy, personal achievement and meaningful contribution.

15.5
WILLINGNESS

---

*"There is a need for a Copernican revolution in the way that human motivation and behaviour change are approached in practice. The dominant approach to these is still focused on how people can be controlled and manipulated to behave or change ... Current knowledge and research has shown that this is based on 'old' science pointing in the wrong direction. Now that we understand how the human organism **naturally** learns and self-organises actions, the future will not be about how motivation can be controlled from without. Instead it will turn on the ways that human motivation is functionally designed and experienced from **within**.*

Edward L Deci[5]

Edward Deci, his colleague Richard Ryan and the research community that contributes to the development of Self-Determination Theory[6], have assembled formidable evidence for the importance of freedom and choice in human motivation. Their essential thesis: **What we do willingly, we do well.**

The focus of the research of Deci and Ryan is the consequence of the genetic need for autonomy. When we feel in control of our own lives: when we are self-determined, free from imposed constraints and free to make independent choices, we tend to thrive. When we contribute willingly, our own powerful intrinsic motivation is the driver of our behaviours. This research ties personal freedom strongly to well-being. When we are willing, we feel well.

On the other hand, when we feel controlled by others: when we are limited or constrained, when our options are limited or when we are behaving unwillingly, then our drive and sense of purpose is weak. Imposed limitations tend to cultivate lethargy.

Now I am not suggesting (and nor are Deci and his colleagues) that the solution is for the staff to do whatever they want. That would be anarchy, an avenue of constant uncertainty. Every person at work knows that, even in the best of jobs, there are some tedious or unpleasant tasks that just have to be performed. However, the research of the Self-Determination Theory community shows us that workers are likely to be committed if the work context and culture encourage:
- Meaningful work;
- Opportunities for personal achievement;
- Individual choices about how to achieve work goals;
- Freedom from excessive supervision;
- Scope to make inputs into how work is organised and performed;
- Personal creativity and initiative.

It's when the volume of imposition becomes pervasive that we turn off from work. In an address to the Glasser Australia conference in 2017, Ed Deci[7] showed a slide full of words and phrases that imply compulsion. He suggested that the consistent use of more than a few of these words in written or verbal communication is experienced as a threat to individual autonomy. Some examples were:

The words and phrases to which he drew our attention are all associated with commands, with orders. Workers who would be committed and willing when given clear direction and reasonable autonomy baulk at directives. Prescriptions such as these undermine our intrinsic motivation:

The figure below, adapted from some findings from a paper by Deci and Gagne[8], illustrates relative levels of perceived control and the resulting levels of engagement:

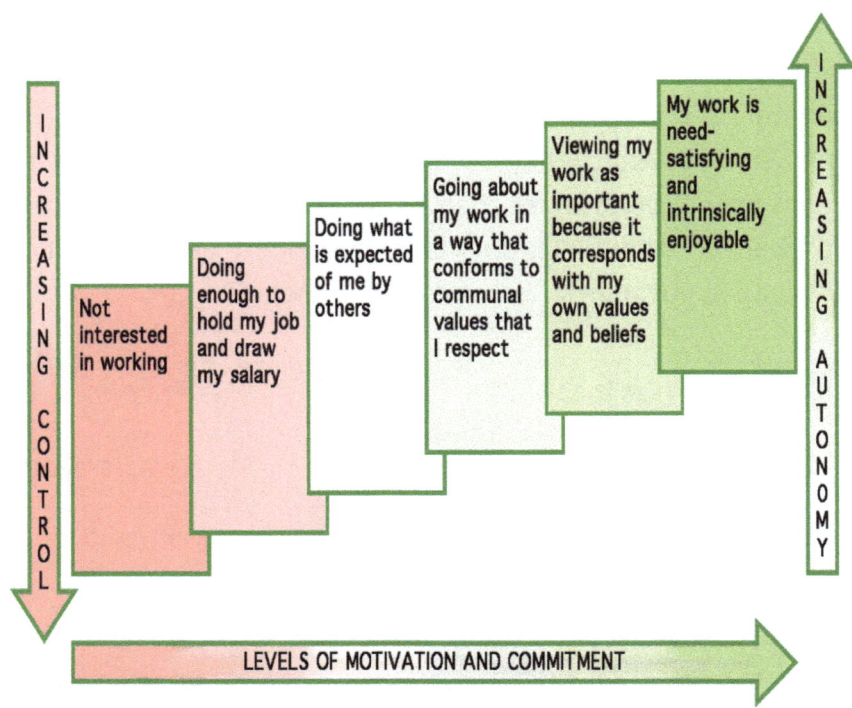

LEVELS OF MOTIVATION AND COMMITMENT

As the figure above illustrates, the feeling of 'out of control', which includes 'going along with expectations that are not aligned with our own beliefs', erodes motivation and commitment. Humankind does not take kindly to being a cipher, a pawn in the game. Our status as autonomous individuals, our free will and our freedom of choice matter to us. When we perceive that our free will is thwarted, our spirit sags.

In contrast, whatever seems worthwhile to us, whatever we see as interesting and important, whatever we can invest with our personal contribution: these things encourage our commitment.

Throughout the body of research collected by Deci and his associates there is the clear message: attempts at controlling motivation misfire; they result in lower levels of internal motivation. This is as true of rewarding to control as it is of more overtly coercive management behaviours. Rewarding a behaviour to 'reinforce' it comes from the 'old science' of human behaviour: the illusion that behaviour is controlled from the outside.

What actually happens when leaders use 'rewarding to control' is that we may do as we are told: work for reward or even accede to threats - if we perceive that the pay-off for compliance is important to us - but our engagement will always be low-level and conditional. Our contrived willingness lasts only as long as the reward is available, or the threat exists. Only when we are pursuing ends that are intrinsically need-satisfying is our engagement sustained. Extrinsic incitements, whether they offer short-term pleasurable benefits or help us avoid pain, don't last.

I observed the effects of external reward being played out in a company that I consulted to for a brief period. The HR department was proud of its bonus system despite the clear evidence that it created dissatisfaction. Senior managers allocated annual bonuses to those who they regarded as most effective. The message that this sent to those who did not receive a bonus was never discussed, even though it was startlingly clear. Relationships between staff members who received bonuses and those who did not deteriorated sharply. Staff turnover (always a problem for this company) accelerated soon after bonuses were announced. There was an increase in lateness and workplace absenteeism. The people who were not rewarded by a bonus received the implied but unstated message: "You are not valued; you are not good enough". Their interest and commitment fell away, and they simply went through the motions of their job or began to look through the 'Ad' columns for other employment.

Did the staff who were 'rewarded' become more committed? I asked them. They said that the bonus they received was just what they deserved for doing what they did. When I asked how they would react if they did not receive a bonus in future, they all agreed that they too would make less effort or look for another job.

Attempts to use rewards such as bonuses, prizes or awards are almost always pernicious. They have 6 un-useful effects:
1. They undermine the individual's intrinsic motivation;
2. They position staff as puppets - mere instruments of their managers;
3. They encourage one-up, one-down relationships between leaders and staff;
4. They damage the network of productive relationships that exists in the company;
5. They distract from the inherent meaningfulness or importance of the work;
6. They isolate people from real contribution and involvement in the organisation.

15.6
CREATING OPPORTUNITIES FOR INTRINSIC MOTIVATION

The alternative to external control is the creation of a context in which the opportunity for internal motivation abounds. Even though we can't motivate our staff, we can deliberately create a culture in which everyone can enjoy personal need-satisfaction. If we pay careful attention to the conditions we create as leaders, we liberate our staff to find enjoyment in their work.

Let's examine the genetic needs in turn and identify the many specific practices that the leader can implement in working towards a culture in which the conditions that support intrinsic motivation are supported. You will see that many of the possible strategic approaches that are related to one need, overlap with practices that may satisfy others.

I am not suggesting that all of these practices are needed in order to enhance employee motivation. What these suggestions offer are some practical ways to identify leadership actions that support engagement and motivation.

15.7
AUTONOMY SUPPORTIVE CONDITIONS

Persuaded by Deci, let's embrace his assertion that an autonomy-supportive environment is the one most likely to encourage willing and self-directed commitment.

To create these conditions, we can:

- Encourage our staff to make a **meaningful contribution** by connecting with them at levels that encourage them to identify with and value the organisation and its goals. When this level of valuing is created by 'Conversation for Alignment'[9], and when staff can make a difference through

their contribution to the conversation, the resulting synergy is satisfying for all involved.
- **Develop** the **expertise** of our staff and defer to it. As we grow their capabilities beyond our own, their unique contribution to the business will bring with it the necessary freedom for them to act in accordance with their acquired knowledge and skill.
- **Offer choices** whenever they are realistic and appropriate. Many businesses now offer flexible negotiated hours, opportunities to work from home, technology to connect employees with an international knowledge community and so on.
- Use **strategies such as the 'Window of Certainty'**© to collaboratively define the boundaries within which staff are expected to work, while allowing autonomy to achieve outcomes and to contribute to the purpose of the organisation in their own way.
- **Empower teams and work groups** to independently create collaborative solutions and innovations for the business.
- **Provide resources** and funding that allow team members to personalise their workstations, offices or classrooms.
- **Encourage individual experimentation** and exploration of strategies and product creation.
- **Endorse our staff to** freely communicate with others in all branches of the business. (This is especially important when the company has a large bureaucracy or many branches). Freedom to converse with all colleagues who can share useful information, wherever they sit in the hierarchy of the business - including freedom to communicate freely with the 'boss' - is a strong indicator of an organisation's effectiveness.
- **Free our workforce from** restrictive work practices, authoritarian supervision or harassment of any kind. Liberate

team members from 'rules' and restrictions that hinder entrepreneurial efforts or personal initiative.
- **Provide enough freedoms** to enable staff to feel that they are the willing authors of their own work life, while providing just enough structure to avoid individual and organisational confusion.
- **Encourage** everyone to take **personal responsibility** for outcomes. This must include freedom to act without securing prior multiple permissions when the agenda of the business is threated.
- **Open avenues of access** to conversations that are related to way the organisation achieves its purpose. This might include opportunity to give technical expertise that relates to important decisions but may also include the way human resources are led and managed.
- **Banish micro-management.** Nothing erodes our sense of autonomy faster than being supervised and regulated every step of the way.

15.8
Achievement supportive conditions

It's almost impossible to feel a sense of personal achievement without enough autonomy to contribute as an individual. When that condition is satisfied, all of the strategies below can enhance the sense of personal competence and contribution:

- **Recognition** of the individual contribution made by each team member. Note that this is different from 'rewarding'. The research shows that affirmations or appreciation by leaders or co-workers are not seen as rewards, so long as they are

embedded in one-to-one or small group conversations. In these contexts, they are perceived as encouraging acknowledgement of work quality. However, if we embed them in a 'formal' ritual such as a weekly staff award, they are likely to be interpreted as 'rewarding to control'.
- **Respectful consultation** and similar signals that each person is making a contribution that counts towards the success of the business.
- **Elevation in status** that is related to the perception of work quality and future contribution.
- **Promotion of those who are capable**, especially when this brings with it a higher level of meaningful access to the organisation's direction and decision-making. There is a good reason why people in leadership roles usually report higher levels of job-satisfaction than those who are overlooked! As leaders, we should always keep this in mind.
- **Removal of one-up/one down**. Practices and communication that convey 'one-up/one down' relationships interfere with our sense of significance. One of the contributions of the field of transactional analysis is that unequal relationships are often interpreted as parent-child interactions. When our team members feel that they are treated like children, they tend to act in a childish rather than a responsible manner. Their sense of being important to the business is diminished.
- **Promotion of the use of helpful feedback or feed-forward.** When staff members receive feedback that informs them, and which they can use to improve the quality of their work, they tend to take strong ownership of their performance. They understand how to be even more powerful contributors to the organisation. Notice that this is different from critical feedback of past performance, especially if no coaching is offered or available.[10]

- **Investment in training.** Offering training experiences which increase the sense of control a person has over their work performance enhances personal power. This is the kind of learning that's seen as useful by the person to whom it is being offered. However, if the learning is perceived as remediation to help the team member 'keep up' with job demands, it has the opposite effect.
- **Giving reasons** for decisions or strategies is empowering. It is not only respectful it is also helpful. When we know why we are doing something, this underpinning explanation boosts the sense of being in control.

15.9
CONDITIONS THAT ENCOURAGE SATISFYING RELATIONSHIPS

There are many kinds of relationships that invigorate us in the workplace. I have appreciated and enjoyed working with colleagues who challenged me, who held me accountable and who tested me with new information or evidence. I have also appreciated those who were straight with me, those who included me, those who worked along-side me through difficulty. What all of these relationships had in common was that the colleague had my best interest (or our shared interest) at heart. We don't need to be friends with our work colleagues to enjoy working with them (although almost certainly we will be friendly towards them - an important distinction). Satisfying workplace relationships do flourish when:
- **There is mutual trust.** We trust our leaders and colleagues when they are honest, predictable, act in our mutual best interest and make a reliable contribution to the work we do together. Our trust in our leaders is always undermined when

we believe that they are pursuing private or selfish agendas, or not telling us the whole truth.
- **Honesty is invested in communication.** This point is related to the last - but goes further. People are more comfortable devoting energy and commitment to an organisation when they are certain about what is happening and why. There is no 'need-to-know' going on in an organisation that is open and honest: no secret executive business.
- **Networks of practice** are created, encouraged and nourished. There are few things as likely to draw individuals to be strong contributors as sharing, discussing their practices and informing each other. Opportunities to learn from each other and bounce ideas around are energising. The model created by the Dreyfus Brothers[11] suggests that once 'knowledge workers' have become adept at their work they learn most confidently from fellow practitioners. In these networks of practice, both formal and informal mentoring arrangements naturally form to support innovation and change.
- **Shared values-in action** are developed. I affirmed the importance of supportive values that are enacted in practice in one frame of the 'Window of Certainty'©. They have also featured in other sections of this book. When everyone in an organisation acts responsibly and respectfully; when support and encouragement are commonplace; when people are kind to each other and considerate of the needs of others, it is a good place to work.
- **Real teams are created.** The kinds of behaviours and the sense of shared purpose that result when leaders deliberately build teams is described in Chapter Thirteen.
- **Perceptual agility**[12] is deliberately taught and promoted. Second Perceptual Position is a powerful practice in any workplace. It supports consideration of others, appreciation

of difference and empathic communication. All of these help our organisation to be perceived as an intrinsically satisfying place to work. Leaders who provide opportunities for staff members to learn and practise the skills that lead to greater understanding of each other have this investment repaid many times.

- **Experiential learning** replaces lectures and media presentations. Workplace learning models tend to be relatively arid: information-rich but lacking in opportunities for processing and interaction. When an organisation introduces modes of learning that encourage participants to discuss, critique and process information, and to actually practise the skills they are learning about, the pay-off is twofold. With this kind of learning understanding and skills tend to be acquired at a deeper level, and the intense professional interaction makes for satisfying relationships.

15.10
CONDITIONS FOR MEANINGFUL LEARNING TO TAKE PLACE

There is some debate about whether learning is a genetic need. Some experts regard it as simply an integral dimension of our humanity. Born almost helpless, humans don't have many behaviours until they learn them. Unlike a foal that can stand within minutes of birth, or a turtle that must accomplish a complex set of behaviours to get to the sea and then already knows how to feed, humans have to learn everything from scratch. To encourage us to learn, we have emotional incitements. Dopamine, a 'feel-good' neurotransmitter, is released in the body both as we anticipate learning and as we become aware of growing in knowledge and skill. William Glasser used to say that "Fun is the genetic reward for learning." The presence of dopamine associated with learning feels similar to the joy we feel from the activities we regard as fun.

As we grow older and enter the world of work, we encounter two kinds of learning:
- The kind of learning that is enjoyable, that enhances our sense of competence and is acquired in the context of supportive relationships. This kind of learning seems meaningful and we get a 'dopamine buzz' from it.
- The kind of learning that is associated with the pressure of other people's expectations. This is 'keep-up', 'must do', 'your career depends on it' learning. This kind of learning generates anxiety. When we are stressed by having to learn in order to survive at work, then cortisol and adrenalin are released into our system instead of dopamine. We do not feel good when that happens.

It is obviously the first kind of learning that is experienced as need-satisfying at work. As leaders, we can optimise meaningful learning and minimise stressful learning through:
- **Building capacity.** This means offering useful learning as company policy. It's 'getting ahead' learning rather than 'keep-up' learning. With this approach staff members come to regard invitations to extend their competence as opportunities for growth, rather than emergencies when new technology is introduced, or the work context changes.
- **Using experiential learning** modes as discussed above.
- **Providing coaching and mentoring** whenever people are working through changes or when they are at transition points

in their career. The availability of this kind of sustained support features in many need-satisfying workplaces.

-Initiating an organisation-wide recognition that **mistakes are logically tied to learning**. Any time that we are faced with something we can learn perfectly at first attempt, it's probably so simple that it's not meaningful. When our staff are learning complex skills, acquiring profound knowledge, or becoming familiar with and implementing revised processes or systems, error is inevitable. When people fear the consequences of making mistakes, learning is inhibited and implementation is sluggish. Team members will thrive in an environment where mistakes are always seen as an opportunity for deeper learning.

- Systematic promotion of **learning that is collaborative whenever possible.** There is a dimension in learning together - about better ways to improve the job our staff do together, - that is more satisfying than solitary study.

- **Encouraging and celebrating personal initiative, creativity and inventiveness.** The 'continuous improvement' initiative which is part of 'The Toyota Way' (their Toyota Production System) produced many small but significant improvements of practice[13]. Constant improvement is part of everyone's job description at Toyota. Front-line workers are encouraged to suggest improvements and help make them. The company has a process for taking worker suggestions to the top level. There is a culture in which participation and contribution are systematically encouraged. Contrast this with a typical tale from a business franchise. A young employee found a way to reorganise the stock room to streamline access to the most used items. His colleagues loved the innovation. It enabled a more efficient use of their time. The business owner told him to put things back the way they were. "Innovation", the young man was told, "is the job of management!"

15.11
Creating Safe Conditions

Feeling safe is a baseline requirement for satisfaction at work. Abraham Maslow[14] believed that self-protection was a manifestation of the Survival need – at the most fundamental level of his 'Hierarch of Needs'. Although we now realise that whatever need that is not being met is uppermost in our minds, it is difficult to experience satisfaction at work if there are perceived threats to our physical and social safety. A pervasive sense of threat inhibits everyone from bringing their 'A' game to the workplace. Nobody thrives if they fear for their physical or social safety.

There are numerous ways of addressing workplace safety, but many of them are misguided. Anti-bullying and anti-discrimination policies and committees abound in schools, workplaces and in public life. They all focus on the behaviour they want to avoid, which draws attention to exactly the wrong thing.

Years ago, it was discovered that posters around the factory that listed dangers actually increased the number of accidents. 'DON'T SLIP' messages at the top of a flight of stairs (accompanied by a banana-skin image) led to an increase in the number of people who obeyed the implicit message 'SLIP'. The mind, for all of its range and power, is very slow to process a negative.

Workplace safety is best served by focusing on what we want. Listing safe, respectful supportive behaviours, discussing them and defining what these look like in action, are far more important than perseverating about the unsafe acts that are the opposite of these. That's why the 'Window of Certainty'© in Chapter Fourteen is focused on values-in-action that make the organisation a safe and satisfying place in which to work.

Workplace safety is enhanced by identifying and defining:
- Respectful behaviour and communication;
- Supportive ways of giving useful feedback to colleagues;
- Avenues for negotiating differences;
- Ways to contribute to the efforts of our colleagues;
- Empathic communication skills.

Other ways to encourage the safe and respectful behaviours in which all staff can thrive include:
- **Creating the clear boundaries** defined by a 'Window of Certainty'©.
- Using **performance management** processes that are future-focused and encourage self-evaluation, such as 'Performance Feed-Forward'© [15]
- Promoting **creative engagement** as opposed to obedience. As discussed above, a culture of compliance is anathema to energetic performance. It also brings with it the feeling that not obeying the rules can get you into trouble. With that as a pervasive background, 'watching your back' tends to become more important than doing your best.
- **Opportunities to influence the future.** Staff members feel safest when they know that they have avenues of input into the future, especially in the domains that will have an effect

on their own tasks and environment. Without opportunities, people can easily feel helpless: victims of decisions and circumstances over which they have no control.[16]

15.12
CONDITIONS THAT ENHANCE MEANINGFUL CONTRIBUTION

Victor Frankl believed (as the title of his seminal work indicates[17]) that an innate need in humankind is the search for meaning - for a dimension that will usher a higher level of significance into our lives. Frankl built the practice of logotherapy on his conviction that this profound (almost spiritual) hunger may be the most important of our genetic drivers. When it is not satisfied, this need leaves us restless and unfulfilled. When we have opportunities to live and work in ways we consider to be meaningful - ways that make a unique contribution to our world - we feel worthy: our self-concept (our affirming identity) is staunchly buttressed.

The importance of meaningful work is also emphasised in the work of Marco Korn[18] - referred to in the previous chapter. Marco's eloquent illustrations show the different relationships (between leader and subordinates) that are created when the leader provides meaningful direction and welcomes the contribution of the staff. When employees are genuinely invited to play a significant role, there is a revolution of status and significance in the way in which the organisation operates. Team members are invited on board as co-creators of the team's success, and initiative emerges from many sources.

When these 'Conversations for Alignment'© are encouraged, professionalism and expertise are accorded the same status as leadership. As illustrated below, the notion of supervisor and subordinate is effectively collapsed in the pursuit of common endeavour.

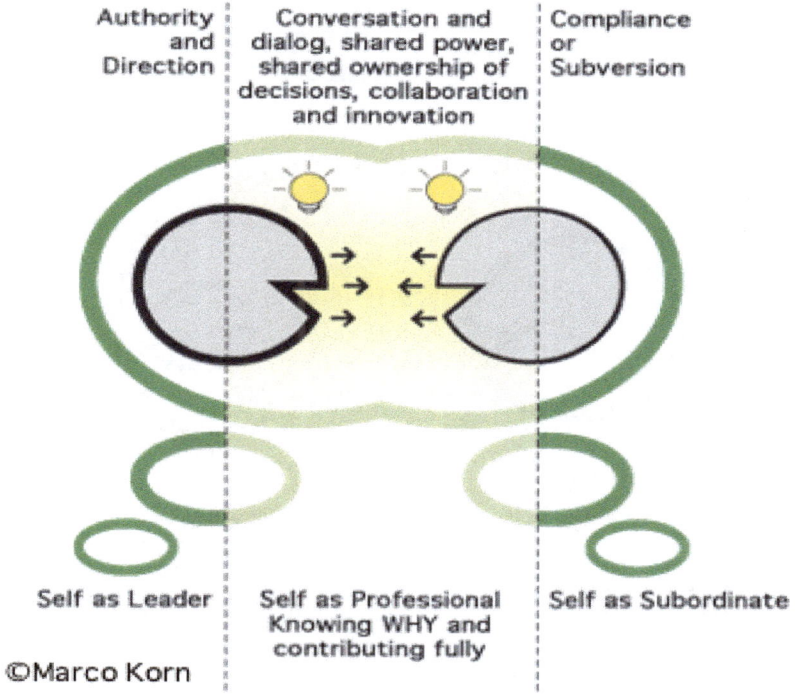

In the diagram on the next page, Marco contrasts the collaborative approach to leader and staff communication with the traditional leader-employee relationship. In a conventional authoritarian relationship the leader is the sole custodian of insight and jealously guards the authority of rank.

When the relationship is authoritarian, as illustrated below - when the leader is a fountain of directives and staff members are simply receivers of managerial wisdom - the staff options and freedoms are few. Marco suggests that the two alternatives are either compliance or subversion. Of the two, active antipathy and the careless undermining of the health of the business can often seem more fulfilling than the grinding sense of submission to disrespectful power.

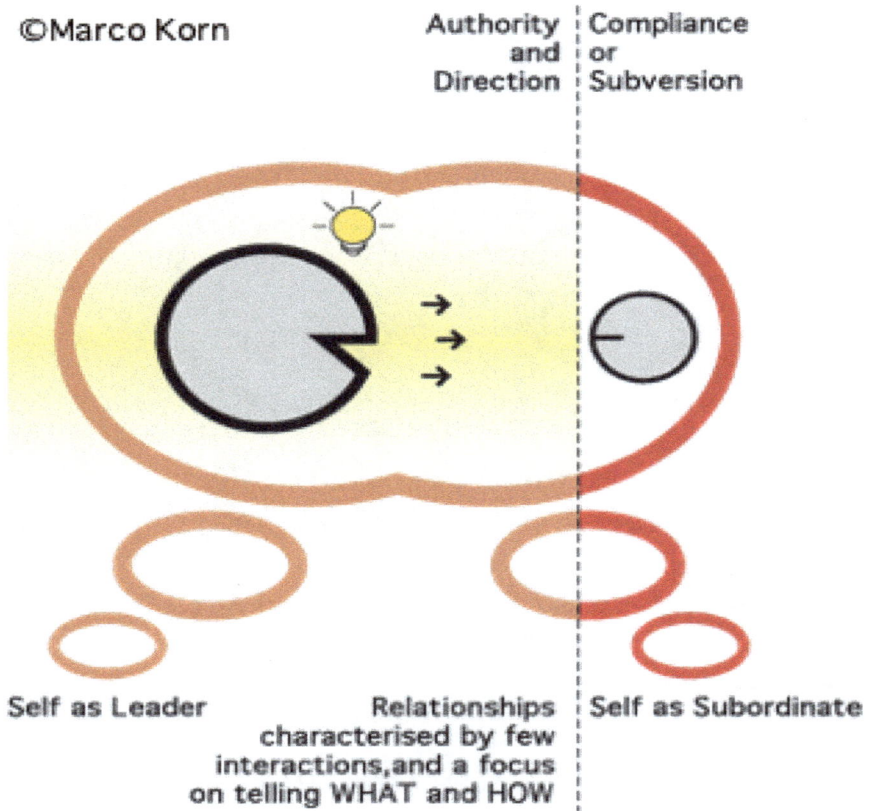

As Victor Frankl maintained, when life is reduced to the mechanics of existence; when the self is felt as making little impact on the workplace zeitgeist, the alternatives are experienced as depression or retreat. When our staff feel that these are their choices, neither option is good for our business!

Being cast in the role of an 'inferior' (juxtaposed with the leader's 'superior' status) engenders some un-useful behaviours. The Transactional Analysis[19] movement described 'one-up' / 'one-down' relationships as the generators of a 'parent-child' dynamic. When we feel that we are being treated as children we tend to display the worst characteristics of childishness: e.g. selfishness, immaturity, carelessness about consequences, laxity and impulsiveness. Inviting these behaviours by treating staff members as 'one-down' makes little sense for a leader.

What Marco Korn's portrayals show is that creating 'adult-adult' relationships is an invitation to responsibility and enterprise. Extending the offer of involvement is a leadership act of potent significance. When the leader accepts the 'paradox of power', and consequently empowers the people upon whom he or she depends to have a stake in the business and to work as co-contributors, then the disparity in status recedes. There is a difference in roles but an equality of importance.

The challenge for leaders is that, even when we can see the pay-off from inviting our staff to contribute meaningfully, it all takes time and energy. This is another element of leadership that requires disciplined mind management. The *Leader-Minded* approach - the kind of thinking that will invest in the future through collaborative practices in the present - is demanding.

As leaders, we can offer meaningful contribution to our staff through organisation-wide practices by:
- Communicating purpose, values and beliefs to provide direction, and by allow skilled and professional staff to create their own 'best way';

- Using the 'Window of Certainty'© approach in every team, as well as across the whole business;
- Validating individual initiative and enterprise by creating avenues for these to be communicated and implemented.
- Encouraging a responsible level of experimentation throughout the business.

This approach to leadership is more than the selection of wise policies and practices: it is willingness to adopt *Leader-Mind*. With this attitude, we can see leadership for what it is: a role not a rank. As in all things, form should be dictated by function. If what we want from our staff is the highest level of personal motivation; that they identify with the WHY of our business and apply their capability to its achievement, then the traditional practices associated with leadership superiority will not suffice.

The creation of an organisation where people will thrive kindles commitment. A working life that allows staff members to feel important, effective, respected, and free to contribute their very best will serve the whole business. When the tide of human motivation is rising across the organisation, because the conditions for it to surge are deliberately being created, then the engagement of the staff will be a sign of leadership effectiveness.

CHAPTER SIXTEEN

AVOIDING DISTRACTIONS!

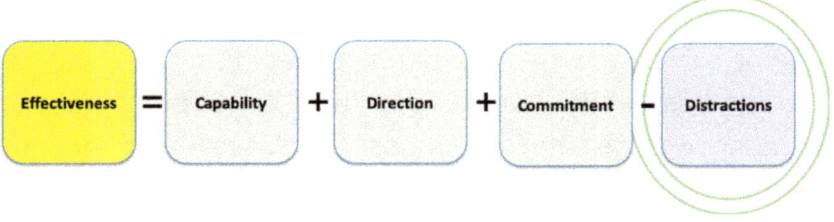

Starve your distractions. Feed your focus

Daniel Goleman[1]

16.1

DISTRACTIONS - HINDRANCES TO UNRELENTING FOCUS

Ah! If only we could make sure that the main thing is always the main thing: If we could attend only to those things that build and utilise the capability of our staff; if we could always take responsibility for improving the situation; if we could always self-evaluate rigorously and live up to the best in ourselves.

Sadly, the human mind for all its incredible strengths is conspicuously distractible. Short-term desires, the tug of our less-admirable emotions; or the ease with which we can find ourselves annoyed with other people - all these constantly intrude. These and a million other intrusions swarm around us like pesky mosquitoes - irrelevancies that are always on the verge of capturing our attention and energy.

The theme of this book has been managing your mind to become the best leader you can be. But it would be unrealistic not to acknowledge the challenges that assail that kind of singular priority.

In this last section, I want to explore some of the most common and potent diversions - the distractions that are most likely to sabotage our leadership effectiveness. I have separated them out, but you may notice that they are all inter-related. Where I can, I will suggest some specific strategies for managing and ignoring these side-tracks. Overall though, you will not be surprised to hear from me that the one global master-plan implicit in the theme of this whole book is the ability to observe, understand and manage your own mental processes: to be acutely aware of what's going on in the labyrinthine miracle of your mind, and how to re-direct it when it's leading you astray.

Some of these potential distractions are more pervasive for some people than others. We all experience our 'fuzzy thinking' in different ways. For that reason, I am not presenting the following hindrances in any order of priority. They are all ever-present, lying in wait to seize the attention of the unmanaged mind!

16.2
POLITICS

Politics is not leadership: it is a temptation for leaders.

Leadership is not political behaviour. It has much higher ends than personal gain.

Politics wins battles, but squanders trust. Leadership leads to the future – it depends upon building and maintaining trust.

One of the definitions of politics offered by my dictionary reads: *'activities aimed at increasing someone's status or increasing power in an organisation'*. Unfortunately, this kind of politics is the one we often experience in our workplace. It is usually associated with getting one's need for power satisfied at the expense of other people. The dictionary does capture this when it refers to the phrase 'playing politics' as 'acting from personal gain rather than principle'.

Because it is focused on 'power over', politics in the workplace is self-serving but never organisation-friendly. When we behave politically, we exploit the vulnerabilities of others; we are not satisfied unless we 'get even'; we conceal our own vulnerabilities and true motives. Leaders who act politically expend energy in protecting and enhancing their own status as 'number one' in their team or in the business generally.

As soon as a leader attempts to elevate their own importance or dominance at the expense of another, they are generating three unhelpful dynamics:

1. They are degrading the importance of others – the antithesis of empowering them. The staff who are diminished by the leader's offensive tactics will no longer make the contribution they could have made.
2. A one-up/one-down relationship is signalled. A parent-child interaction is almost always the result.
3. There are winners and losers - the powerful and the defeated. The interactions and communication become dysfunctional as Karpman illustrated in the Triangle of Blame[2].

The antidote to the temptation of political behaviour is Fourth Perceptual Position. As leaders, when we ask ourselves "What do I really want? short-term domination or long-term leadership effectiveness?", we are reminded that our effectiveness depends on the capability and commitment of others. If we adopt the *Leader-Mind* perspective and think: "Will this organisation be better served by enhancing this relationship or damaging it?", then we are most likely to eschew politics.

16.3
BEING STUCK IN SELF

In First Perceptual Position you will recall that we are acutely aware of self. Our thoughts seem right to us; our emotions can keep us in thrall; our physiology helps or hinders, and our actions seem eminently justifiable.

When we are paying attention only to ourselves, we are blind to other people, and to the bigger picture. It's not that First Position is unhelpful of itself. Self-referencing is critical to our identity, and to integrity under pressure. It enables us to be helpfully assertive and assists other people to understand us. Being in First Perceptual Position is not a problem: getting stuck in 'First' is internal myopia - a very unresourceful state!

When we get stuck in self, our thinking is narrow but does not seem to be. Our total state - that mix of thought, feeling and physiology - locks us in place. We easily enter the Self-Defeating Spiral[3], that condition where our perception is restricted by an *idee fixe* or a momentary obsession. Of course, when our thinking is limited in his way, we easily draw unhelpful conclusions, take action on these conclusions and then justify our behaviour by referring to them.

To those around us, when we are stuck in First Position, we seem needlessly stubborn. We tend not to notice what is obvious to others. None of this is good for our credibility and effectiveness as leaders.

The antidote to 'stuck in self' is an unfaltering preoccupation with perceptual agility. At any time when we are sure we are right, and we notice that we are not paying attention to the people around us, we should activate perceptual agility: switch off our attention to self; ask ourselves: 'What are other people around me thinking and noticing and why? What would an objective observer be noticing? What's in the best interest of our team or our business?'

Using perceptual agility, the mindful habit of deliberately paying attention by using all four ways of viewing the world liberates us from getting 'stuck in self'.

16.4
THE HEADY WINE OF HUBRIS

Suffering from hubris is another way of becoming locked in First Position – and of overestimating the significance of whatever is playing through your own head.

The danger inherent in believing in your own superiority is that it's based on two unwarranted assumptions:
1. That some people are superior, or that their knowledge is superior - not just different, better.
2. That you are that superior person.

What almost always accompanies such hubris is that the opinions of others, the knowledge that they share and the advice that they give are discounted. A leader whose arrogance isolates them from the opinions of others sheds the authority of influence and surrenders their right to lead.

In my own case, the temptation of self-importance, even conceited self-delusion, was often present. It was only held in check by an important piece of mind-management that I acquired early in my leadership journey. When I sensed that my stream of pride was about to burst its banks and overflow into pomposity, I would recite the 'Humility Poem' to myself.

I can't recall who taught me the poem. I know that my version differs from the original, which is attributed to, *Saxon N. White Kessinger* (1959) and is said to be displayed on a bronze plaque attached to a building at the Rochester Institute of Technology in New York. But as it runs through my head, this is how my version of the poem goes:

Some time when you're feeling important;
Someday when your ego's in bloom;
The moment you take it for granted
You are clearly the best in the room;
Whenever you think that your going,
Will leave an unfillable hole
Just follow these simple instructions
In the interest of peace for your soul.

Take a bucket and fill it with water,
Plunge your hand in it up to the wrist,
Take it out and the hole that's remaining
Is the measure of how you'll be missed!

You may splash all you please when you enter,
You can stir up the water galore.
Take your hand out: you'll see an instant,
The water's as calm as before.

Pay attention, be grateful and value
What the colleagues who work with you do.
Success is hard work and good fortune,
And the work of the team, not just you!

Having a mantra like this has the capacity to keep us centred. If you detect in yourself the warning sign of a sense of superiority, I invite you to commit the 'humility poem' to memory and recite it as often as needed.

Whenever you are feeling important, whenever your ego's in bloom ... recite the poem to yourself. It should leave you suitably grounded!

16.5
WRIGGLING FROM RESPONSIBILITY

Failing to take responsibility to do whatever we can to improve, remediate or salvage situations is a contagious workplace disease. If we as leaders succumb, then it will be found everywhere.

Evading responsibility comes with the familiar cast of behaviours: blaming, complaining, finding fault, self-excusing, criticising others and hollering for help.

"It's not my fault", "The dog ate our business plan", "It's not fair" and "Somebody should do something" are the symptoms that sing through the corridors of our school or business when evasion-of-responsibility sickness grips it.

The central problem is that evading responsibility is always stuck in the past and the problem instead of attending to the future and the solution. No difficulty is ever overcome by finding out who was responsible and blaming them. No mess is ever managed by complaining about its origins and meting out retribution.

It doesn't matter whether there is a fault to be found, or whose fault it was. The only thing that matters is "What do we do next?" And then, when the situation is improved or the problem solved, we might usefully ask; "What did we learn?" and "How can we avoid this happening again?"

When the leader of a team or organisation models the acceptance of responsibility and takes action, a clear and positive signal is sent to the rest of the firm: "When we see a problem – we solve it".

No person, however powerful and creative they are, can ever step into the past. When something has happened, it is in the past. All the things we can do to improve our organisation will be done in the present or the future. Certainly, we can learn from the past - but not in order to apportion blame. The reason for working out what went wrong is to work out what we can change now or in the future.

The advice given to Anne Mulcahy[4], a former CEO of Xerox is relevant to all of us. When things go wrong she was told, there is an order of priority: "When the Cow is in the ditch you have to do three things. First get the cow out of the ditch. Second, find out how the cow got into the ditch. Lastly, make sure that you do what's necessary so that the cow doesn't fall into the ditch again!" Notice what is important here. There is no mention of apportioning blame; of finding out whose fault it was that the cow got into the ditch. The attention is all on the future.

Blaming is such an energy-sapping, disengaging, wasteful activity. If you are a human being, you will make mistakes. If you employ people or have a team, they will make mistakes. Do we want to learn from these flaws, or spend time identifying, blaming and sapping the spirit of someone who erred?

Leaders build capacity when they take responsibility and then act. The resilience formula A.C.T.S.[5], as articulated by Ali Sahebi and augmented by Judy Hatswell, applies here: it is as useful to an institution as it is to a person. When something goes wrong, we should take these four steps:

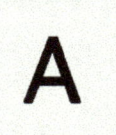

Accept the situation.
Whatever happens, or whatever someone else has done, there is no point in blaming, complaining or demaning excuses.
None of us has the magic wand with which to go back into the past and make changes. What is done is done. We are leading powerfully when we take responsibility for finding a solution.

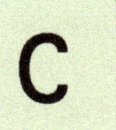

Consider the CHOICES you have.
However profound the problem, there are always choices. Our leadership is eloquently demonstrated when we focus on "what next?". As Victor Frankl observed: *"Life ultimately means taking the responsibility to find the answer to the problems it presents".*

Take Action.
Decisions are only really made when action is taken. It's important to move into the solution space by taking action as soon as possible. Almost all difficulties are exacerbated by inaction. "Let's move on and improve" is the way to recover. Take action, even if it does not work out perfectly.

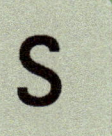

Self-Evaluate.
This is the learning step. What did we learn from what went wrong? Every learning organisation learns from blunders and miscalculations. When the focus is on identifying what to do next time, on improving the future, on how to build capacity - then the business will thrive.

Accepting responsibility is such an effective leadership behaviour because it is (if not uncommon) unusual enough to be unexpected! Any reader of the news can see the truth of this writ large in the headlines of the business pages. The response of senior executives to downturns or scandals is so often to make excuses or to blame more junior leaders. The effect of this on the organisation's morale is often seen in declining future results.

Whenever we take responsibility, we are leading. What we model will be adopted by others. A culture in which every person knows that the right thing to do is to step up and fix things will enhance any organisation or institution. When leaders take responsibility, everyone else does!

16.6
LIKING AND DISLIKING

Years ago, a wise mentor told me that 'disliking' people was an excuse for treating them badly. The complement to this proposition is that 'liking' people is a justification for treating them favourably. For the leader, both these poles of interpersonal valuing are fraught with stumbles.

Even though social media has trivialised the notion of 'liking', the danger implicit in the act of preferring some people to others and thereby treating them differently is easily observed. Even a hint that the boss has favourites, or 'less-preferred' people, undermines the perception of the leader's integrity. Trust is eroded.

Like most leaders, I found the expectation of personal neutrality a challenge. We all find it more natural to be in rapport with some people than with others. Like-minded colleagues are pleasant to deal with. Those with very different perceptions or beliefs often represent a challenge to our tolerance and acceptance. However, despite the intuitive difficulties of this reality, it presents some serious mind-management issues.

A slightly bitter colleague sighed as he once told me (having been damaged by some accusations of bias) that: "The only safe way is to treat everyone badly; to be a grumpy boss. That's so much easier to sustain than trying to be nice to everyone!"

I don't agree with his conclusion, although I can empathise with the pain that led him there. A better solution would be to maintain an amiable neutrality towards every member of your team: to be friendly towards (but not friends with) your work colleagues; to develop a habitual set of accessible, courteous and tolerant behaviours - whatever our intuitive response to the person might be.

Once again, this is a matter of the 'want' we pay attention to; what we are putting on the scales of our personal decision making. If our leadership effectiveness is our priority, then even-handedness comes more easily because every individual's contribution to the business matters. Everyone's personal capabilities and commitment matter. It is worth effort on my part to influence their willingness to become vested in the purpose and goals of the organisation.

When this is our priority, we can make the effort to manage our thinking and actions to ignore the emotional tug of natural rapport or apparent incompatibility.

16.7
INDULGING OUR EMOTIONS

We are humans - an emotional species. As Glasser[6] pointed out, there are four elements of our behaviour, like the four wheels of a car. We can steer our total behaviour well if we manage our thoughts and actions well. Our back wheels - our emotions and the concomitant physiology - are drivers of our energy levels but unreliable navigators.

As we steer a course along our leadership journey, we will inevitably experience a full range of emotions: sometimes we will feel up and sometimes down; sometimes optimistic but often-time depressed or anxious. And it's much easier to act with energy and commitment when we are feeling buoyed by internal sunshine than when the emotional drizzle sets in.

Once again, the way to manage this roller coaster is to stay on our front wheels: to recognise our back wheels as a natural but sometimes unhelpful distraction. Because we know that all behaviour is total, the four wheels of our behaviour naturally synchronise with each other. Just as it's more difficult to be energised if our back wheels are signalling misery, so it's hard to feel down for long when we are acting constructively and thinking about solutions.

Of course, it's unwise to ignore our emotions. They do give us some useful indicators about how we are travelling. Sometimes they are reminding us that we are too stretched, working too hard, failing to consume the nutrients of personal capability. Without enough rest, enough recreation, enough connectedness and 'me-time', we all falter eventually. But heeding the signals that we are over-committed and indulging their effects on our leadership are two different things.

Peter, one of my early bosses, was a striking example of the effects of indulging his emotions. His was a kind of bi-polar leadership. To borrow from a children's rhyme: "When he was up, he was very, very, good. When he was down, he was horrid". Inevitably, it was his down times that came to define him in the eyes of his staff.

If we are to be leaders with well-managed minds, our plan will be to pay attention to the information we are getting from our back wheels, but never to indulge them; never allow our feelings (good or bad) to manage us. When we are effective, we will always be shifting ourselves onto our front wheels, guided neither by euphoria nor misery, but always by the task of building capability, pursuing success, engaging the energy of our team.

16.8
SELF-PROTECTION

Self-protection is a formidable distraction. It's the human survival instinct tuned to the jungle of the workplace. It's the 'watch you back' mentality, the fear of being caught out by a mistake.

Self-protection flourishes in a work environment in which there is a leadership focus on management by exception: catching people doing wrong. The firmer the grip that policy, procedures and bureaucratic systems have on the workplace, the more likely that it will be accompanied by the vigorous growth of 'safety first' thinking.

In this kind of context, compliance and conformity is the norm. Institutional cortisol floods the arteries of the organisation. Taking risks, initiative and creativity are discouraged. Attention to purpose is abandoned in favour of personal safety.

Of course, this kind of thinking is facing $180°$ from the lifeblood of every organisation, school or business. It's focused on the 'don't want' rather than the 'really want'.

Your team or company will thrive on opportunity sought and taken: on the free play of personal striving and responsible creativity. Any institution that is not prepared to push against the boundaries of present practice is either flat-lining or declining. Opportunistic risk-taking is a requirement of future success. Self-protection sabotages all of this.

The cure for a culture of self-protection is to confront it with contradiction: to validate risk-taking and experimentation by celebrating mistakes as an opportunity for learning. The epicentre and example of this shift in thinking has to be in the offices of the executive. When the leaders of an organisation seek opportunity rather that watch out for error; stop watching their backs and start to search for and encourage the fragile shoots of new thought and action, this change of thinking ripples through the organisation.

16.9
THE BLINDNESS OF BOSSES

A significant distraction in any organisation is created when the executive leader or executive team does not really know what is going on. The result is that decisions are made on the basis of unclear or inaccurate information. There are no good choices without good information!

It's easy to create this particular distraction. All that needs to happen is for the leaders in an organisation to make it clear that bad news is unwelcome.

In any firm there is always a mixture of bad news and good news: problems as well as profit; complications as well as improvements. Knowing about all of these - the setbacks as well as the advances - is a requisite condition of thoughtful leadership and management. If the true situation is not known, if only the successes are communicated to them, the leaders are working blind.

Most people know this. Most leaders would recognise it as an issue. Yet it's startlingly common to hear of leaders who get angry or upset and 'shoot the messenger' when they hear bad news. This is especially likely to occur when the news that is conveyed includes indicators that it is the boss's own strategy or communication that is causing a problem!

Two mid-level school leaders in a recent workshop told me: "We know that our Principal is harming morale. We know specifically what the problem is. We could easily help him to address the situation. We know we should – but we're not brave enough. He would turn on us and accuse us of disloyalty if we were to tell him what he really should know." One of them went on to say: "The problem is that I find myself doing the same thing. When one of my staff reports the result of one of the boss's indiscretions, I probably make it clear that I don't want to know. I can't address it. It's too hard - so I usually just brush them off."

This is the way that selective communication becomes a disease that permeates the whole organisation. Everyone tells their leaders and managers only what they think their supervisor wants to hear.

The antidote is simple. Warren Bennis[7] uttered a truth without price when he famously opined that "If I had to reduce the responsibilities of the follower to a single rule it would be to speak truth to power!"

It goes beyond this though. It is the leader who must model the cure for the disease. The first duty of every leader is to assure his or her followers that they are expected to 'speak truth to power': that however unwelcome the message, the messenger will always be welcomed. Then the second job of the leader is to walk their talk. Everyone in the organisation will hold their breath until the first really bad news is conveyed to the boss. Only when the information is greeted with thanks and appreciation, and the concern is calmly and openly addressed, will everyone know that their leader's word can be trusted.

16.10
LINEAR THINKING

I have recently been teaching my eight-year old grandson to play chess. He is at the stage where he knows the moves, has some good simple strategies but tends to focus only on the next move.

Predicting the consequences of our next action - and preferably the result of these consequences - is essential in leadership, as it is in a game of chess. In my workshops I use a teaching activity called 'traffic jam' that illustrates the dead ends we can get into by only thinking one move ahead.

In systems language, trying to go from a problem to the first solution that comes to mind is linear thinking: a belief that the solution can be reached one step out from a problem. This is the kind of thinking that, for example, addresses a fall in sales by cutting back on staff, with the result that production falls and customers go looking for a more reliable supplier. Complex problems require complex solutions.

Peter Senge[8] writes sagely about the antidotes to linear thinking in 'The Fifth Discipline'. The 'Fifth Discipline' to which the book refers is systems thinking: the ability to see the circular nature of the systems we create and their consequences, and to anticipate the effects of actions. I don't have the space to explore this further, but I recommend Senge's book to anyone who needs to cure themselves of the distraction of linear thinking.

16.11
THE SYSTEMS TRAP!

Systems thinking may be the cure for linear thinking, but systems themselves can be a distracting inefficiency in any organisation. Sometimes the procedures we set up – call them systems, policies or processes – are not fit for purpose (often because linear thinking is embedded in them).

We create systems and processes to provide predictable ways of managing recurring situations. Instead of having to invent the solution every time, we just implement the system or the policy. But what if the process we adopt creates problems?

Let me give an example: performance management processes can often create massive distractions in a business, school or other enterprise. There is an abundance of research[9] that shows that performance management processes are often inefficient and ineffective. They are spawned by a kind of 'common sense' thinking that actually makes little sense.

A business that I worked with took it for granted that if they did not 'monitor' the performance of their workforce then people might not work hard. Through their HR department, they introduced quarterly reviews. The review took the form of a questionnaire that required staff to describe their work practices, identify any aspect of the work that they were having difficulty with and also one way in which they were attempting to improve their own performance. Once HR had analysed their answers, the next step was an interview with their line supervisor.

However, the line supervisors generally found the interviews time-consuming and difficult, so they often either did not happen or were held less frequently than intended. Despite this, the questionnaires still kept coming every quarter.

HR complained to the line managers who responded that the results they were getting were too complex, and that receiving simpler data might make the interview process more efficient.

HR responded by buying a computer program that staff could use to input their answers. This also saved the HR department from the difficult job of analysing the questionnaires: let the computer do it!

The staff inputs were analysed by the program and a one-page report was generated that purported to show areas of concern (red flags); areas for improvement (purple flags); and areas where the employee was performing as expected (green flags). The reports looked very pretty. The program also incorporated data such as sales figures, customer complaints and so on.

Not surprisingly, the interviews did not increase in frequency. When they did happen, supervisors tended to focus on red flags. In the absence of training, they did not know what else to do. Nobody looked forward to these interviews. They were hated equally by both line managers and staff!

The staff soon worked out the computer program. They did not identify aspects of their work that they were finding difficult: why call down red flags upon themselves? They also only identified areas for improvement that were safe. The computer never forgot if they said they were trying to improve something, so it was easiest to identify work practices that they had already mastered. In that way, they would keep scoring green flags. They also noticed the kind of data that the computer kept and made sure that they attended to this information as a priority.

The net results:
- Staff spent hours inputting data and working out what kind of inputs would make them look good. (Did I forget to mention that the computer automatically spat out lists of employees who were eligible for a bonus?);
- Work practices were skewed away from what was best for the company and towards whatever would most successfully game the system;
- Supervisors relied on whatever the computer told them instead of being connected enough with their staff to know about their performance, where they needed help to improve or what their real strengths were. Performance interviews became perfunctory: "Here are your red flags, green flags. You did not get a bonus";
- Under this regime, relationships between staff and their line managers deteriorated; the staff themselves became disengaged. There was little creativity or initiative in the way they went about their work.

Now I may be accused of choosing an extreme example, but I assure you that it's not. Distractions of this kind abound in large and small organisations. In large organisations, unwieldy HR practices are often the source of such distractions. In smaller businesses, centralised decision-making or elaborate sign-off protocols slow down the business and discourage initiative. In schools, monitoring and administrative processes that have nothing to do with educating the children proliferate and sap the teacher's energy and time. In bureaucracies, the distance between the leaders and the people who deliver the product, means that productive dialogue is minimised and that there are lots of demands for compliance (a very low form of engagement as we have seen.)

The solution? The solution is for the leaders of the organisation to focus ruthlessly on purpose, and to ask searching questions of every system or practice that occupies the time of the staff: What is the intent of this business? Do these systems complement our purpose or distract us from it? Do these practices really build staff capability and commitment? Is energy directed to where it is most productive?

I will leave the last word on this to repeating Peter Drucker's[10] advice:
"There is nothing so useless as doing with great efficiency that which need not be done at all."

16.12
NOT TRAINING FOR TOMORROW

The last distraction we will consider is common, pervasive and predictive. It is the dead end of being too busy managing the present to prepare for the future.

One of the key dimensions of organisational effectiveness is building capability for now and the future, because the future does not take care of itself.

Like so much else in life, this is an exercise in our ability to delay gratification. Allocating hours to mentoring, coaching, training, or blue-sky speculation; initiating opportunities for collegial discussion to encourage initiative and enterprise - these rarely have a short-term pay-off.

Not getting around to these things always has long-term consequences. If we don't build capability, the capacity of our organisation (and of individuals within our enterprise) will be static. Not developing our people is a self-fulfilling invitation to organisational decline.

'Leaving a trail of capability in their wake' is the hallmark of effective leaders. It takes time, it takes energy, it requires foresight, but it is always a telling investment.

When we are immersed in the busy-ness of the moment, lifting our heads to notice that we are doing things that we could train other people to do is a requisite act of leadership. Realising that there is an untapped capacity for more to be achieved when each and all of our staff can act with even 1% more knowledge and skill is visionary work. It's leaders' work.

As we noted earlier, building capability never stands alone. When our colleagues see themselves as growing in proficiency and status, they increase their commitment to the organisation that nurtures them. Their engagement creates a culture of expectation: the expectation that everyone thrives here.

One of the saddest things I hear from leaders is an unhappy commentary on their own lack of foresight. They say "What's the point of training people? When they are more skilled or know more they leave for a better job!" These executives don't realise that what those who move on leave behind them is a culture of possibility; a culture into which other people will step expectantly.

I think it was Ken Gilbert[11] who pointed out to me that organisations can choose to be where the staff go to learn, flourish and advance - or where they go to moulder and decline.

When there is no opportunity to grow, our staff may be there for life, but the dead hand of 'hope denied' infects the workplace. Energy is leaked from the system.

Conversely, when the members of your team see their colleagues grow in competence and skill - and see that they have the same opportunities - the message is clear: 'This organisation gives us scope to grow'. When their associates move on to better jobs or are promoted within the business their own confidence and resolution are ignited. They perceive that the implications for them are: 'This team will provide opportunity'. 'I can hope to flourish here!'

CHAPTER SEVENTEEN

CONCLUSION

"If your actions inspire others to dream more, learn more, do more and become more, you are a leader."

John Quincy Adams[1]

17.1
ONE LIGHTHOUSE OR MANY CANDLES?

In our work as leaders, it's often as important to know what we can't do as what we can do: to be aware of our limitations and how to allow for them. Being appointed to a leadership or managerial role brings with it no special anointing of flawless judgement. Relying on a self that we know to be fallible and sometimes myopic is a waste of the resources we could construct around ourselves. If we hope to transcend the limits of our own mind, we have to reach beyond self and embrace the wisdom of the people we lead. As Drucker[2] notes, we should focus on our contribution rather than on our own achievement: on the potential we ignite, not the gleam of our own lamp.

I was reminded of this a few years ago while watching some children unwittingly enact a fable for the *Leader-Minded* :

It had been an unusually warm, clear day in the South West of Wales where my wife and I happened to be staying at a small country golf club. The soft light of evening was blowing gently to a close in the late sea breeze.

Children spilled about the place as their parents gathered on the terrace and in the bar sharing their afternoon stories. As it grew dark, I noticed that the smaller children were clustered in an almost invisible hollow, surrounded by longer grass and protected by a rock slope. As the darkness spread, first one - then a little procession - of the children left the hollow and then re-emerged from the clubhouse clutching the tiny flickers of 'Tea-light; candles, begged from the grown-ups inside.

The first few cupped their hands around their flame, shielding their fragile glow from the strengthening breeze. But over the uneven ground leading into their sheltered nook, one-by-one they let their attention slip from the candles and the tiny flames flickered out in the wind. Back they went to the few who were still standing in the protection of the building to relight their candles from those whose flames still burned. There was a fierce conversation about what to do.

This time, all the children huddled together; they turned inward towards their candles. They moved deliberately slowly, the lights sheltered by both cupped hands and the barrier of their tight formation. Over the difficult ground they shuffled, feeling their way - intent on protecting the tiny flames.

Some candles did wink out during their shuffled passage, but immediately the whole group stopped and huddled even more tightly together, until the dark wick was re-kindled by another flame.

Soon all the children were all in the hollow - the warm glow of their many candles casting flickering shadows, the warm light making their enchanted hollow a place of mystery and excitement. The chatter and laughter and energy grew; excitement spilled into the evening.

Sadly, the spell was shattered! An older child emerged from the club house and from her lofty 11-year-old perspective announced: "You can't possibly see properly out here. Come straight inside to where it's properly light". Reluctantly they complied. Flames flickered out and excitement died as the chastened group adopted the new truth and shuffled obediently back into the steadily monotonous light inside the building. The night lost its sense of possibility and the hollow became invisible in the dark.

Reading some Australian statistics about the perception of bosses by the people they manage, I was reminded of that evening. A *'Business-on-Line' survey in 2012* [3] discovered that:
- *55 % of leaders believe their ideas are the best and do not listen to others;*
- *45 % of leaders assume they understand the problem when they don't;*
- *50 % of leaders don't listen effectively;*
- *50% don't read other people's reactions well;*

- *48 % of leaders leave meetings without a plan for what to do next.*

These kinds of figures are repeated again and again in research about the effectiveness of leaders. They are a huge challenge to the leader-centric myth of how to get the best from our organisations. If we build our enterprise around ourselves as the one beacon of rightness - the one lighthouse of initiative - we are forgetting that our primary purpose is to bring hope and enlarge capability: to light the candles around us. It is those with whom we surround ourselves who will create the blaze.

In a work environment where competitive edge is usually only temporary, the idea of the one right answer from the top is redundant. When innovation and willingness to adapt and change are required, leaders who are able to see themselves as lighting the spark in others come to the fore. The time of the leader as the sole beacon, gathering their staff obediently into that light, is no longer. And which of us, in our wisest thinking, really believes that we alone have the only good ideas, the only right answer?

The children in the hollow were on to something! When they wanted to solve a problem they gathered together, lighting the flame for each other in order to create a sense of shared excitement and possibility. The energy that emanated from their hide-away was palpable and self-sustaining. It was only extinguished by the arrival of the 'big sister' who gathered them all into the 'proper' light.

The energy I had observed was important I realised: because it's not just an organisation's capacity to re-invent itself that is at stake here. There is also the growing understanding that the style of leadership that disregards the initiative of employees has a profound impact on the organisation's bottom line.

A recent survey from the Gallup Organisation[4] *concluded that the behaviour of leaders account for the majority of variance in almost all performance-related outcomes. Management styles that lead to worker disengagement affect productivity, profitability, customer satisfaction and absenteeism.*

It seems increasingly that the leader who chooses to stand bathed in the light of his or her own importance is driving the energetic participation of their employees out of the business: and they are reducing accessible effectiveness in great volumes.

Looking for hope in this dismal picture, I find myself turning again to the children who were lighting the flames of excitement and possibility into the light as they passed on the fire from their candles.

Jack Zenger and Joseph Folkman published convincing evidence In the Harvard Business Review blog in 2012[5] *that the better the leader, the more engaged the staff.*

Zenger and Folkman are not specific about what it is that the best leaders do. In the pages of this book I have teased out my own answers from a tapestry of personal experience and a life of leadership learning.

In '*The Leader-Mind Equation*' I have provided a template for leaders who are willing to grasp that their greatest opportunity is to build the capability and harness the capacity of their co-workers. Those who are *Leader-Minded* know that even when they are not themselves able to inspire the flames of involvement, intellectual engagement and creativity in their staff, they are always giving room for the multiple other lights in their organisation to blaze.

In a forest, the seeds that fall in the shadows of the most dominant trees usually fail to thrive. There is too little sunshine; the gloom is pervasive; the nutrients are leached from the soil by the needs of the giant tree that has to feed its own looming height and spreading grandeur. The forest extends and thrives by giving room and opportunity for the new growth among the smaller trees where the beams of sunlight are not so scarce, and the where soil still has nourishment to spare. If you are tempted to be a big tree, it's time to re-think. Your job is to give the little trees room to grow! [6]

17.2
THE EFFECTIVENESS FORMULA

The effectiveness formula that created a framework for these pages is not complicated. It embraces both what leaders do and their capacity to leave a legacy.

Its elements are relevant to our own performance as leaders, and to our leadership vocation: to enhance the effectiveness of those we lead.

The Leader-Mind Equation

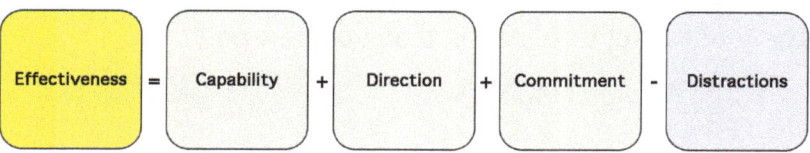

To become an effective leader requires the unfaltering development of the personal capabilities needed to provide clear direction and a compelling purpose for our team. It impels us to learn how to engage and influence so that the motivation and commitment of our workforce is optimised. So that time and energy are protected, leaders - if they are wise - learn to deflect, minimise or ignore distractions.

Because we all depend on our workforce for productivity and performance; because leaders can't achieve alone; these same essentials are the constituents of the development of those that we lead.

When we methodically and thoughtfully develop the capability and capacity of our staff; connect them with lucid and well-reasoned aims and direction, then they can draw on their own internal drivers in the service of the organisation.

When we secure their commitment by shaping a workplace with a need-satisfying and meaningful culture; when we manage and minimise the myriad potential distractions that assail every organisation - then our colleagues will learn and thrive.

Understanding and applying this formula instigates the adoption of *Leader-Mind* : the practice of comprehending, mastering and ordering your own mental processes in order to be the most effective leader that you can be.

17.3
ARE YOU WILLING?

"Do or not do. There is no try."

Yoda[7]

The information anyone needs to develop *Leader-Mind* is freely available. In the last 30 years, knowledge about how the mind functions has moved from the domain of the psychology professional to the public sector. Anyone who is willing to read the relevant books[8] or attend courses in Choice Theory[9] can acquire all of the knowledge required. I have done my best to communicate the essence of that knowledge in the pages of this book.

The biggest barrier to learning how to manage your mind effectively is not knowledge - it's will: willingness to take the responsibility for using what you know. Mind-management requires discipline because it's not what you know that matters - it's what you do with that knowledge!

Everything that we do to manage our mental processes is predicated on an act of will. Our unmanaged minds tend be lazy; to seek the shortest path to need satisfaction. In life in general, it's easier to give in to short-term expediency than to think long-term. In the stressful busy-ness of work it's easier to blame and complain than to take responsibility; it is less of an effort to behave impulsively than to accept the challenge of acquiring *Leader-Mind*.

I used a modern parable to open this book. An allegory about a device that can help us to be far more effective than we could ever hope to be without it. I will return to the story of this device and its powerful applications in this conclusion.

Each of us has access to a device that is capable of improving our lives and those of others. This device, the human mind, is an instrument with extraordinary power, capable of astonishing feats of insight. It can capture and use the data we receive from the world around us. It can apply itself with subtlety and dexterity to bringing hope and inspiration to the people we lead, and to the organisations we serve.

But using the device and its features is a purposeful and effortful enterprise. In the hands of a careless user, its power can be squandered by distractions. We can twitter away its potency in a shroud of trivial activity.

Our minds - those amazing but easily diverted instruments of cognition - are served best when they are tended attentively. We use our minds most aptly when we take the time to know how our mental processes function so as to be alert for the traps and detours. Our minds serve us well when we manage our self-talk and imaging; when we learn to identify what we want and how to achieve it.

I have named the disposition to use our thinking and behaviour in the enterprise of leadership as *Leader-Mind*. Developing and employing *Leader-Mind* in a thorough and intentional way will help you to be the most effective leader you can be. Using any of the *Leader-Mind* practices I have described can be your initiation to a journey of effectiveness - in leadership and in life.

If you take on the challenge to use the information that I have shared in these pages - in order to manage your mind and your life - you will be accepting personal responsibility for your leadership effectiveness.
A scary thought?
A huge opportunity!

Rob Stones
June 2020

Notes and References (by Chapter)

Introduction
1. It is one of the many ironies of leadership in practice that making mistakes is often regarded as if it was a defect: to be avoided if possible or denied if not. Conversely, the research clearly points to the incidence and acceptance of mistakes and bad decisions as an unavoidable formative experience for those who will go on to be successful. Despite this, all too many leaders try to hide their mistakes and justify their poor decisions. I am embarrassed to admit that at times I was guilty of this myself. The anomaly in this is that leadership competence improves with learning. Avoiding or denying error is incompatible with learning. Nobody can learn to do something new or better without willingness to embrace the inevitability of mistakes while they are still learning.
2. Haruki Murakami, *What I Talk about When I Talk about Running*, Knopf, 2009.

Chapter One
1. RG Pierre is my sometime alter ego. I have used 'him' as a nom-de-plume and occasionally appeared in his guise. It's RG whose thoughts often appear in my notebooks, often surprisingly unbidden! Any time I offer a quote from my notes that seems to have no link to my systematic thinking, I tend to attribute it to RG.
2. I have adapted the definition of Leadership Capability that I learned from Dr Malcolm Davies, CEO of 'Learning at Work' (Brisbane). In his article *Unlocking the Value of Exceptional Personalities*" he defines leadership as: *The capable use of a set of learnable skills to influence oneself and others, to set aside purely personal interests to contribute to the achievement of group goals.*" The article is included in a collection by Robert. E. Kaiser: *The Perils of Accentuating the Positive*, 2009.

3. Victor Frankl, *Man's Search for Meaning*, 1952.
4. William Glasser MD, *Choice Theory, A new Psychology of Personal Freedom,* 1998.

Chapter Two
1. John C. Maxwell, *Good Leaders ask Great Questions,* 2015.
2. *The Paradox of Power* and the *Law of Reliance* first appeared in workshops and articles created by FutureShape Consulting in 2015.
3. Michael Fullan, *Leading Quality Change,* workshop notes 2011.
4. Peter F. Drucker is often regarded as the founder of the career of management. In his writing he makes it clear that what he describes as management is often what we would describe as leadership. Drucker's range of insight and practical wisdom has been the inspiration for many of the ideas in this book.
5. Max DePree, *Leadership is an Art*, 2002: "The first job of a leader is to define reality. The last job of a leader is to say: 'Thank you'. In between, a leader must be a servant and a debtor."

Chapter Three
1. Warren Bennis, *On becoming a Leader*, 1989.
2. 'The various forms of the *'Leader-Mind'* matrix are sometimes referred to as the 'FutureShape Leadership Framework'. I have used this framework for fifteen years to illustrate the way in which self-knowledge and self-management are the heart of leadership effectiveness.
3. Warren Bennis, *On becoming a Leader*, 1989.
4. RG Pierre is often responsible for the author's most sensible utterances!
5. Lin Yutang was a Chinese inventor, linguist, novelist, philosopher, and translator.
6. Jean-Paul Sartre, *The Psychology of the Imagination* (1940)

CHAPTER FOUR
1. Barnes Boffey, *Reinventing Yourself*, 1993.
2. Although our brain processes data that exists outside ourselves, the brains hardware is independent of the events and people who exist around us and with whom we interact. All of the processing is internal - inside ourselves.

   The phenomenon of mind, the mental experience of what is going on in our neural biology, is the way we access this brain activity. And the interactivity of brain (the neural structures) and mind (our awareness) is total because they are indistinguishable by the persons in whom their operations occur.

   More simply put, we make sense of our experiences through internal mental processes. There is brain activity that corresponds with these, but all that we are aware of are the mental processes through which we access experience.
3. William Glasser MD, *Choice Theory, A new Psychology of Personal Freedom*, 1998.
4. Self-Determination Theory or SDT brings together a number of theories about human motivation that explore the different effects of internal and external motivation. Edward L Deci and Richard M Ryan are its foremost researchers and proponents. The scope and significance of SDT can be explored through the website: selfdeterminationtheory.org.
5. NLP or Neurolinguistic Programming has several variations of name due to the various proponents of NLP wanting to incorporate their brand into the name. NLP is a 'trail of techniques' that exploit the connections between language, thought and brain activity. Many of the pre-suppositions of NLP are compatible with and included in the psychological theory that is presented in this chapter.
6. David Rock is a prolific writer who is the director of the 'NeuroLeadership Institute'. Rock is the author of the S.C.A.R.F.

model that is referred to later in this section, and his writing offers many other insights into the need for leaders to be thoughtful about the mental activity of those they lead.

7. Norman Doidge, *The Brain that Changes Itself*, 2007. Doidge provides numerous examples of the brain's plasticity. His research and writing refute the popular beliefs about the limited adaptive capacity of the adult mind.

8. Positive Psychology includes all of the research and writing that promotes the understanding and optimisation of the healthy mind. The origins of traditional psychology were derived from a medical model based on diagnosis and treatment of mental 'illnesses'. Positive Psychology takes a different approach: it focuses on what we can do to enhance the capacity and resilience of healthy minds.

9. English 'Public Schools' are anything but public! In Australia we would call them 'private' schools. The name is a hangover from their years of establishment which predated the time when attendance at school was universal. The archetype for these schools (usually boarding schools and originally mainly for boys) included many practices that we would now think of as somewhat barbaric: at the time they were usually regarded as 'character-building'.

10. As an adult who is now a professional communicator, I now wish I had developed a very different attitude to the Latin that I was taught. Because this ancient language provides the etymology for many of the words we now use, it would be really helpful to have the same level of command and insight into these derivations as my wife Valerie has. Fortunately, she edits my work and therefore compensates for my ignorance!

11. My colleague Judy Hatswell introduced me to the terminology of 'internal references' to describe the positive pole of the brain's comparing process.

12. William Glasser MD, *Choice Theory, A new Psychology of Personal Freedom*, 1998.

13. William Glasser MD, *Choice Theory, A new Psychology of Personal Freedom,* 1998.
14. Abraham Maslow was the ground-breaking author of the 'hierarchy of needs' model and one of the first professionals to ascribe human behaviour to need-satisfaction. Maslow described the needs as: survival, safety, love and belonging, self-esteem and self-actualisation. Dr Glasser drew on many of Maslow's ideas, but challenged the primacy of the survival need because some people do take their own lives when other needs are not being satisfied *or* risk their own survival to satisfy their needs for power or fun.
15. William Glasser MD, *Choice Theory, A new Psychology of Personal Freedom,* 1998.
16. Edward L Deci (with Richard Flaste), *Why We Do What We Do,* 1995.
17. Daniel Pink, *Drive: The Surprising Truth About What Motivates Us.*
18. Victor Frankl, *Man's Search for Meaning,* 1952.
19. Victor Frankl, *Man's Search for Meaning,* 1952.
20. Edward L Deci (with Richard Flaste), *Why We Do What We Do,* 1995.
21. David Rock, *SCARF: a brain-based model for collaborating with and influencing others,* 2008.
22. Abraham Maslow, *A Theory of Human Motivation,* 1943.
23. Chade-Meng Tan, *Search Inside Yourself: The Unexpected Path to Achieving Success, Happiness,* 2012.

Chapter 5

1. *David Bohm, Thought as a System* (from the transcript of a seminar held in Ojai, California from 30 November to 2 December 1990).
2. George Miller, a cognitive psychologist developed a number of theories about memory. What he called 'The Magic number 7 (plus or minus two)' illustrated the limited capacity of short-

term memory. Most adults can store between 5 and 9 items in their short-term memory. We now know that his theory is imprecise in a number of ways. However, his finding that we can actually pay attention to and hold in memory only a very few things is generally accepted.

3. People filter the information that enters their perceptual system by Deletion, Distortion and Generalisation. We **delete** by ignoring, overlooking or tuning out what we regard as unimportant, or which is threatening to our established ideas. **Distortion** is the personal prejudice that twists our perceptions: we see things as we want to see them. **When we generalise** we apply a conclusion based on limited experiences to the totality of experience.

4. There is a growing body of evidence that many of our beliefs have a shaky foundation. Read for example Robert A. Burton: *On Being Certain: Believing You Are Right Even When You Are Not.* 2008, Burton demonstrates convincingly that certainty is a mental feeling state that does not equate with objective 'truth'.

5. Stephen S. Covey, *The 7 Habits of Highly Effective People*, 1989.

6. Alfred Korzybski established the field of *General Semantics* in which he argued that human knowledge of the world is limited by both the nervous system and the limitations of language. His famous dictum 'the map is not the territory' referred to his belief that humans cannot experience the world directly but only via their personal interpretations (maps) of the world as they perceive it.

CHAPTER SIX

1. William Glasser MD, *Choice Theory, A new Psychology of Personal Freedom*, 1998.

2. William Glasser regarded the car metaphor as his most useful and insightful contribution to the popular understanding of the working of the human mind.
3. Daniel Kahnemann, *Thinking Fast and Slow*, 2011.

SECTION THREE
1. VINCE LOMBARDI was the coach and general manager of the Green Bay Packers American Football Team and an inspirational speaker. Because of his attitude and success, he became a symbol of single-minded determination to succeed.

CHAPTER SEVEN
1. From my notes of an address by Glen Gerreyn in 2007. Glen is a motivational speaker who is the founder and CEO of The Hopeful Organisation. I think I am quoting Glen, but it may be my summary of what he said.
2. M. Scott Peck, *The Road less Travelled*, 2008.
   Yogi Berra was baseball player and manager who became famous for his idiosyncratic ways of expressing the truth as he saw it. My very favourite is *"If you come to a fork in the road, take it"* but *"If you don't know where you are going, you might wind up someplace else"* is a close second!
3. Daniel Kahnemann, *Thinking fast and slow* 2011.
4. Judy Hatswell of 'Judy Hatswell and Associates' describes and teaches the process of positively reframing a 'don't want' to a 'want' as ***flipping***. It's a succinct and expressive word to describe a positive alternative to a negative perception.
5. Dr Glasser explained that our motivation comes from comparing what we want with what we perceive. He used the metaphor of a set of scales to explain this. When we are in balance, our needs are satisfied and what we want and what we are perceiving are a match. When there is a mismatch between what we want and what we perceive to be happening, the scales are tipped and an urge to change behaviour is created.

6. Emil Zatopek was a Czechoslovak distance runner who was famous for his inelegant running style, his phenomenal training regime and his feats in the 1952 Olympic Games. After winning the 5,000 metres and 10,000 metres he entered the marathon (his first) and won that too! Not surprisingly he was one of my running heroes and I was privileged to meet and talk with him after some fellow runners and I gate-crashed a Czech embassy function in 1967. The embassy staff were keen to eject us but Colonel Zatopek (as he then was) embraced our impudence and we spent a magical half-hour talking about our mutual love of running.

Chapter Eight

1. Actor Will Smith features in a You Tube Clip *Fault Vs Responsibility,* 2018 (published by 'Epic motivation'). This quotation is from the text of his monologue.
2. M. Scott Peck, *The Road less Travelled,* 2008.
3. Stephen Karpman developed the idea of the Drama Triangle and published his first paper on it in 1972. Karpman was a student of Eric Beirne, the father of the transactional analysis movement. The Karpman Triangle is widely recognised as an archetype for dysfunctional social interaction.
4. Edgar Schein, *Organisational Culture and Leadership 5th Edition,* 2016.

Chapter Nine

1. Tad James lists this as the 11th Presupposition of NLP in his *NLP Master Practitioner Training Manual,* July 2004. As Tad James presents it, this presupposition reads "There is ONLY feedback! (There is no failure, only feedback.)". The presuppositions of NLP seem to vary in number depending on the author or trainer presenting them. They all offer embedded assumptions that are useful in acquiring *Leader-Mind.*
2. William Glasser MD, *Reality Therapy,* 1965.

3. Judy Hatswell enhanced Glasser's reality therapy coaching model by adding procedures for 'flipping' to the positive want, and spiralling to achieve clarity about the 'real' or deepest level of want. These procedures, implicit in many of Glasser's demonstrations of Reality Therapy, contribute to the effectiveness of coaching.
4. Jamie Smart, *The Little Book of Clarity*, 2015.

SECTION FOUR

1. Friedrich Nietzsche was German poet, philosopher and composer whose work influenced many other philosophers and writers. Some of his most profound thoughts are often repeated and attributed to the people who quote him (such as: "Whatever does not destroy us makes us strong" and "He who has a why to live can bear almost any HOW").

CHAPTER TEN

1. Albert Camus was a French citizen who was born in Algeria. A journalist, author and philosopher, he won the Nobel Prize for Literature in 1957. Camus is famous for his writing about the meaninglessness of the universe. Nevertheless, he is the author of one of my favourite sayings: "In the depths of winter, I finally learned that within me lay an invincible summer."
2. Norman Doidge, *The Brain that Changes Itself*, 2007.
3. Gary Player: Gary was a South African golfing champion who was renowned for his determination and dedication.
4. M. Scott Peck, *The Road less Travelled*, 2008.
5. Emotional self-management and emotional self-control are two of the seven dimensions of Emotional Intelligence identified in the GENOS E.I. model developed by Ben Palmer. GENOS assessments differentiate between 'Emotional self-management' (managing your ongoing emotional state) and

'Emotional Self-Control' (the ability to control strong emotions). These - like all the other dimensions of emotional intelligence - are important leadership dispositions.
6. Robert Dilts, *A Brief History of Logical Levels*, 2014.
7. Robert Dilts, *A Brief History of Logical Levels*, 2014.
8. Barnes Boffey, *Reinventing Yourself*, 1993. This powerful process encourages a coachee to identify what their feeling, physiology, thinking and acting are like when they are in an unresourceful state. They then describe what would prefer to be thinking and doing, and what emotions and physiology would serve them in the same circumstances. When they have a clear picture of how they would like to be in that preferred state, they adopt the behaviours associated with it.

CHAPTER ELEVEN
1. Robert Conklin, *How to Get people to Do Things*
2. The Perceptual Positions have developed from pioneering work by Gregory Bateson on the different perspectives from which we can view the world. Bateson believed and taught that wisdom depends on the ability to view the world through many lenses. These ideas were further developed by Richard Bandler and Judith De Lozier as the 'Perceptual Positions' or perspectives.
The importance of perceptual agility - the ability to move between the perceptual positions at will – has been identified by the author as a key leadership skill.

CHAPTER TWELVE
1. This is another of RG Pierre's unbidden contributions to the author's occasional scribbling.
2. The coaching procedures I describe here are known as the 'Positive Outcome Process'©, an extension of the WDEOP 'procedures for change' as described by Robert Wubbolding and based on a therapeutic process of 'Reality Therapy'

developed by Dr. William Glasser. The 'Positive Outcome Process'©, was an evolution of these procedures created by Judy Hatswell of Judy Hatswell and Associates.
3. Stephen Karpman, *The Drama Triangle*, 1968. More information is available at: www.KarpmanDramaTriangle.com.

Chapter Thirteen

1. Kenyan Proverb. Although I lived in Kenya for many years as a child, I did not learn this proverb at that time. I first heard it only a few years ago. However, it does resonate with me because it fits in with the wealth of common-sense wisdom that is part of the culture of Africa. My favourite saying from this genre is one I heard often from my ayah as a child: 'An empty pot makes the most noise!'
2. Alex Pentland, *The New Science of Creating Great Teams*, Harvard Business Review 2012.
3. Bruce Tuckman, *Development sequence in small groups*, 1965.
4. Patrick Lencioni, *The 5 Dysfunctions of Team*, 2002.

Chapter Fourteen

1. Patrick Lencioni, *The 5 Dysfunctions of Team*, 2002.
2. I was fortunate to be present when Marco Korn presented his *Conversations for Alignment* model to a group of professionals in 2008. With his permission I have shared this model widely ever since. Marco's work is always appreciated by my workshop groups because it combines deep insight with very clear images! [Marco Korn, *Conversations for Alignment*].
3. Peter F. Drucker wrote so comprehensively about leadership and management that it is rare to find a book on leadership that does not refer to or expound on his ideas. So widespread and perceptive was his writing that more than one leadership writer has commented that most 20th century writing on leadership and management is simply a series of footnotes to Drucker.

4. David Rock, *SCARF: a brain-based model for collaborating with and influencing others*, 2008.
5. Rob Stones; Judy Hatswell, *The Window of Certainty - Defining what you want in your school. Exploring the difference it makes*, 2016.
6. Margaret Wheatley, *Relationships: The building blocks of life*, 2006.

CHAPTER FIFTEEN

1. Gary Hamel: from a presentation on *Continuous Management Innovation* – Fortune Innovation Forum, November 2006.
2. Gary Hamel: from a presentation on *Continuous Management Innovation* – Fortune Innovation Forum, November 2006.
3. The classification of people who work from their personal knowledge and skill as 'knowledge worker' was first coined by Peter Drucker in his book *The Landmarks of Tomorrow* (1959). Knowledge workers can be broadly viewed as anyone whose work output is dependent on their knowledge.
4. In Thomas H. Davenport's '*Thinking for a Living*' (2005) he expands on the idea of the 'knowledge worker' and the motivation of individuals who can be so described.
5. From the foreword to *Self-Determination Theory: Basic Psychological Needs in Motivation, Social Development and Well-Being*, by E.L. Deci and R.M. Ryan 2018, Jan 2000.
6. Self-Determination Theory is described by Deci and Ryan as an approach to human motivation and personality. Richard M Ryan and Edward L. Deci, *Self-Determination Theory and the Facilitation of Intrinsic Motivation, Social Development and Well-Being*, 2008
7. Edward Deci was a keynote speaker at the William Glasser Institute Conference in Newcastle, Australia in 2017.
8. Marylene Gagne and Edward L Deci, *Motivation to Work*, in the Journal of Organisational Behaviour, 2005.

9. Marco Korn, *Conversations for Alignment*, as presented in 2008.
10. Feedback is NOT 360° instruments. I am qualified to use many of these instruments, but no longer do so because they can be misleading and sometimes harmful – even when administered by a qualified practitioner. We know from our understanding of how the mind works that allocating scores and then interpreting them involves two sets of subjective filters: the knowledge, values and beliefs of each person completing a survey; and the knowledge, values and beliefs of each person receiving the results. The potential for misunderstanding and misinterpretation is overwhelming. Leaders are sometimes attracted to the use of these surveys because it seems that they or their staff can receive feedback without anyone having to wrestle with the difficulty of actually owning the opinions expressed in the result.

    The secret of providing useful feedback is the intention. If we want to help our colleagues improve the quality of their future work, we must be prepared to tell them openly what needs to be improved and why - and then use coaching or mentoring to help them improve.
11. Dreyfus S.E and Dreyfus H.L, *A 5-stage Model of Skill Acquisition*, 1980.
12. Refer to Chapter Eleven. Perceptual Agility is a concept developed by the author from the Perceptual Positions – the way we direct the attention of our perceptual system.
13. 'The Toyota Way' is a production system that is grounded in continuous improvement. One of the keys to the success of the Toyota process has been commitment to 'pulling innovation' from front-line workers, rather than 'pushing' improvement from the top.
14. Abraham Maslow, *A Theory of Human Motivation*, 1943
15. *Performance Feedforward* is a conversation-based model for

Performance Management developed by Rob Stones and Judy Hatswell (based on an original idea by Susan Mayes). The Performance Feedforward process offers a structured conversation through which team leaders can discuss goals, progress and aspirations in a supportive and encouraging environment.
16. Stephen Karpman's writing and illustrations show how the attitude of 'victim' is pervasively damaging, not only because of the debilitating effects of personal helplessness, but also because of the effects on the other relationships in the workplace.
17. Victor Frankl, *Man's Search for Meaning*, 1952.
18. Marco Korn, *Conversations for Alignment*, as presented in 2008.
19. Transactional Analysis developed by Eric Berne examines a person's relationships and interaction as a basis for understanding their behaviour. Although derived from Freudian principles, many of the TA insights into relationships are useful in the workplace context.

Chapter 16

1. Daniel Goleman is the author of *Emotional Intelligence* and many other books related to the management of the mind. This quote is attributed to him in *calm.com*
2. Stephen Karpman, *The Drama Triangle,* 1968.
3. I constructed the 'Self-Defeating Spiral to explain the way in which, having formed a strong opinion we tend to look for evidence to support that opinion and ignore any other information. The spiral is usually self-defeating because it takes us further and further from the 'reality' of the situation and usually damages relationships.
4. This advice was given to Anne Mulcahy - former Chairman and

CEO of Xerox - by a plain-speaking and streetwise businessman at a business breakfast. He told her: "When everything gets really complicated and you feel overwhelmed, think about it this way. *"You gotta do three things. First, get the cow out of the ditch. Second, find out how the cow got into the ditch. Third, make sure you do whatever it takes so the cow doesn't go into the ditch again."*

5. A.C.T. – Accept the situation. Examine the choices you have. Take action. This powerful acronym constructed by Dr Ali Sahebi (a Clinical Psychologist and Senior Faculty members of the William Glasser Institute), supports resilience in all circumstances. The hardest part of any difficult situation is acceptance. It's very human to wish fervently that circumstances were different. Taking this first step - accepting the situation - opens up the road to recovery. The S step (self-evaluate) was added by Judy Hatswell.
6. William Glasser MD, *Choice Theory- A New Psychology of Personal Freedom,* 1998.
7. Warren G Bennis, *On becoming a Leader*, 2009.
8. Peter Senge, *The Fifth Discipline: The Art and Practice of a Learning Organisation*, 1990.
9. Many Performance Review and Development Systems do more harm than good!
The first impediment to the effectiveness of these programs is that they ignore the human emotional response to being formally evaluated and given feedback. Research findings in the comparatively new discipline of neuroscience confirms what cognitive psychologists have been saying for years; that people respond negatively to the perceived threat involved in appraisal processes. The result is that they often do not dispassionately process the feedback given to them and, when the feedback is not positive, tend to disengage from the organisation and the manager's influence.

Secondly, these processes make assumptions for which there is contrary evidence. They assume that there are reliable metrics that assist the identification of good and poor performance'. In practice, most 'objective' assessments of performance do not reliably identify performance differences. For example, the Corporate Executive Board Research on Performance Management in 2013 found that two-thirds of employees who receive the highest scores in a typical performance management system are not actually the organisation's highest performers. Finally, most performance review processes are more focused on classifying employees than on encouraging their growth Because of the time commitment required for performance reviews, most businesses succumb to the temptation to put appraisal, staff development, reward systems and managing conversations together in the one system Coens and Jenkins, (*Abolishing Performance Appraisals: Why they backfire and what to do instead*, 2002) found that appraisal is overloaded with too many functions - often one function undercuts another (for example, the focus on reward (or lack of it) interferes with people hearing even positive developmental feedback).
10. Peter F. Drucker, as published in an article titled: *Managing for Business Effectiveness* in the Harvard Business Review, May 1963.
11. Ken Gilbert of Growing Edge Consulting Service, Brisbane, Queensland.

Chapter 17

1. John Quincy Adams was the 6th President of the United States and a renowned diplomat.
2. *The Essential Drucker – Selections from the Management Works of Peter F Drucker,* published 2020.

3. A "Business-on-Line" survey in 2012 discovered that most managers lack basic interaction skills and that employees feel managers damage their self-esteem. A study of 5,000 Australian executives over 10 years came to the conclusion that their leaders can singlehandedly reduce productivity. The research looked at executive skills in relation to team meetings, coaching, delegating and their general ability to communicate effectively ... and it found them wanting.
4. A recent survey from the Gallup Organisation in the USA concluded that the behaviour of managers accounts for the majority of variance in almost all performance-related outcomes. Management styles that lead to worker disengagement affect productivity, millions of dollars every year in profitability, customer satisfaction and absenteeism. The same organisation's worldwide State of the Workplace Report Found that in the USA, Canada, Australia and New Zealand less than one third of working men and women said that they were highly engaged and enthusiastic about their work, with large numbers actively disengaged, passively or actively resistant and making a minimum contribution to their workplace. And lest we be tempted to think this survey only applies to blue-collar workers, the results show that, as education levels rise, disengagement increases!
5. *Are You Sure You're Not A Bad Boss?* Zenger and Folkman Harvard Business Review Blog, August 2012.
6. A metaphor narrated by Daryl Butler, a School Principal who is a Geographer by training.
7. Yoda, the wise elder statesman of the Star Wars movies, uttered this priceless insight in *The Empire Strikes Back*, Episode V of the Star Wars series.
8. Reading suggestions for internal control psychology include:
    - William Glasser MD, *Choice Theory - A new Psychology of Personal Freedom*, 1998.
    - William Glasser MD, *Take Charge of Your Life*, 2011.

- Edward L. Deci, *Why we do what we do*, 1995.
- Lisa Feldman Barrett, *How emotions are made: The secret life of the Brain*, 2018.
- Daniel Pink, *Drive. The Surprising Truth About What Motivates Us,* 2009.
- Daniel J. Siegel MD, *Mindsight*, 2012.

9. The William Glasser Institute offers 4-day Intensive Training in *Choice Theory and Lead Management*. The institute is known in Australia as 'Glasser Australia'. The training can be located through the website www.glasseraustralia.com.au You can also source training through the international arm of the William Glasser Institute https://www.wglasserinternational.org/

Lightning Source UK Ltd.
Milton Keynes UK
UKHW022233300720
367449UK00007B/72